Neurodiversity and National Security

How to Tackle National Security Challenges
with a Wider Range of Cognitive Talents

CORTNEY WEINBAUM, OMAIR KHAN, TERESA D. THOMAS,
BRADLEY D. STEIN

Prepared for the Office of the Secretary of Defense
Approved for public release; distribution unlimited

NATIONAL DEFENSE RESEARCH INSTITUTE

For more information on this publication, visit **www.rand.org/t/RRA1875-1**.

About RAND

The RAND Corporation is a research organization that develops solutions to public policy challenges to help make communities throughout the world safer and more secure, healthier and more prosperous. RAND is nonprofit, nonpartisan, and committed to the public interest. To learn more about RAND, visit www.rand.org.

Research Integrity

Our mission to help improve policy and decisionmaking through research and analysis is enabled through our core values of quality and objectivity and our unwavering commitment to the highest level of integrity and ethical behavior. To help ensure our research and analysis are rigorous, objective, and nonpartisan, we subject our research publications to a robust and exacting quality-assurance process; avoid both the appearance and reality of financial and other conflicts of interest through staff training, project screening, and a policy of mandatory disclosure; and pursue transparency in our research engagements through our commitment to the open publication of our research findings and recommendations, disclosure of the source of funding of published research, and policies to ensure intellectual independence. For more information, visit www.rand.org/about/research-integrity.

RAND's publications do not necessarily reflect the opinions of its research clients and sponsors.

About This Report

This report provides research and analysis for national security leaders, managers, and employees who seek to better understand neurodivergence and neurodiversity and who desire simple and implementable steps to achieve neurodiverse inclusivity for their workplaces. *Neurodivergent* is an umbrella term that covers a range of cognitive diagnoses, including (but not exclusive to) autism spectrum disorder, attention deficit disorder and attention-deficit/hyperactivity disorder, dyslexia, dyscalculia, and Tourette's syndrome. The purpose of this study was to understand the benefits that people with neurodivergence bring to national security; the challenges in recruiting, working with, and managing a neurodiverse workforce; and the barriers in national security workplaces that prevent agencies from realizing the full benefits of neurodiversity.

The research reported here was completed in July 2022 and underwent security review with the sponsor and the Defense Office of Prepublication and Security Review before public release.

RAND National Security Research Division

This research was conducted within the Forces and Resources Policy Program of the RAND National Security Research Division (NSRD), which operates the RAND National Defense Research Institute (NDRI), a federally funded research and development center (FFRDC) sponsored by the Office of the Secretary of Defense, the Joint Staff, the Unified Combatant Commands, the Navy, the Marine Corps, the defense agencies, and the defense intelligence enterprise. This research was made possible by NDRI exploratory research funding that was provided through the FFRDC contract and approved by NDRI's primary sponsor.

For more information on the RAND Forces and Resources Policy Program, see www.rand.org/nsrd/frp or contact the director (contact information is provided on the webpage).

Acknowledgments

This study would not have occurred if not for the leadership of Suzanne Wilson Heckenberg, President of the Intelligence and National Security Alliance (INSA), and Ali Berman, INSA Policy Intern. Suzanne and Ali began a public discussion about the role of neurodiversity in intelligence. The conversation had already been taking place in various corners of the community, and their publicizing of this issue led to this study being funded. We thank them and INSA for their support and assistance during this study.

This study was a collaboration with the MITRE Corporation, and we thank MITRE for its participation. MITRE management supported coauthor Teresa Thomas in her participation of this study, and she brought a depth of experiences and expertise to this topic.

We thank Molly McIntosh for her unwavering support of this research. We thank Danielle Smith, Anita Szafran, and Kristin Leuschner for their assistance conducting our literature review and revising and editing this manuscript. We thank Anthony (Tony) Vassalo for helping to shape the initial design of this study. We thank our peer reviewers Steve Silberman and Susan Straus. Their thorough review of our sources, methods, findings, and discussion greatly strengthened the end result, and any remaining errors are our own.

Finally, we thank the dozens of interview participants who shared their experiences with us, and, in many cases, demonstrated great vulnerability in talking with us about experiences in which they described being harassed and bullied. We hope this report leads to a better future for them and others who will follow in their footsteps.

Summary

National security organizations need highly skilled and intellectually creative individuals who are eager to apply their talents to address the nation's most pressing challenges. Government officials and industry representatives describe the high stakes of the national security threats facing the United States; the demand for a STEM-skilled[1] and technology-savvy workforce; and the need to fill jobs that require enormous attention to detail, precision, and a low tolerance for errors.[2] In public and private discussions, officials and experts addressed the need for *neurodiversity* in the national security community. They described missions that are too important and too difficult to be left to those who use their brains only in *typical* ways.[3]

Neurodivergent is an umbrella term that covers a variety of cognitive diagnoses, including (but not exclusive to) autism spectrum disorder, attention deficit disorder (ADD) and attention-deficit/hyperactivity disorder (ADHD), dyslexia, dyscalculia, and Tourette's syndrome. Neurodivergent individuals are already part of the national security workforce. They are serving as intelligence officers, engineers, security clearance investigators, military service members, and more. Some are senior managers, and it is likely that some are high-ranking executives. However, many of these individuals do not openly acknowledge their neurodivergence for fear of discrimination and bias, and some actively attempt to hide their neurodivergence, sacrificing energy that could be directed at their mission while relying on the talents their differences provide.[4]

U.S. national security organizations, including the military services, intelligence organizations, and the Departments of Defense, State, and Homeland Security, face an ongoing recruitment and retention challenge. These organizations need more people in general, and they

---

[1] STEM stands for science, technology, engineering, and mathematics.

[2] Intelligence and National Security Alliance (INSA), K2Workforce Neurodiversity NatSec Network Kick-Off Event, May 23, 2022; National Reconnaissance Office government official, interview with the authors, June 2, 2022; Office of the Director of National Intelligence government official, interview with the authors, June 14, 2022.

[3] Our choice of terminology, the definitions we use, and our scoping decisions regarding which diagnoses we included and excluded from this study are explained in Chapter 1. We understand and respect that the language related to these topics evolves and can be controversial. We strove to select the most widely accepted terms and definitions at the time of publication, while realizing that language is fluid as society changes.

[4] Office of the Director of National Intelligence government official, interview with the authors, June 14, 2022; National Counterterrorism Center government official, interview with the authors, June 14, 2022; National Reconnaissance Office government official, interview with the authors, June 2, 2022; INSA, K2Workforce Neurodiversity NatSec Network Kick-Off Event, May 23, 2022; NotchbackFiero, "I'll get tested after I retire. Not worth losing my wings over, unfortunately," Twitter post, June 24, 2022; J. C. Lundberg [@jclundberg], "The nuclear Navy would fail if we had comprehensive autism testing in the accessions pipeline," Twitter post, June 23, 2022; Papasmurf811, "Some of us are diagnosed. The military just dosen't know it. I was told by my recruiter not to mention it at MEPS." Twitter post, June 23, 2022.

need candidates with specific skills or who can work at specific locations.[5] The purpose of this study was to understand the benefits that people with neurodivergence bring to national security; the challenges in recruiting, working with, and managing a neurodiverse workforce; and the barriers in national security workplaces that prevent agencies from realizing the full benefits of neurodiversity.

To carry out this research, we conducted a review of primary, secondary, and commercial literature; we conducted semistructured interviews and held discussions with government officials, researchers and advocates for the interests of neurodivergent populations, and representatives from large organizations that have neurodiversity employment programs; and we synthesized findings from across these tasks to describe the complex landscape for neurodiversity in large organizations in general and in national security specifically.

Key Findings

Neurodiversity, like other forms of diversity, can strengthen a national security organization. Fundamental strengths that are common among the neurodivergent population can include pattern recognition, analysis, visualization, problem-solving, memory, and achieving a state of hyperfocus to complete a project—skills that can be beneficial in many fields of interest to national security.

Within the U.S. government, neurodivergent diagnoses are treated as a disability. This policy position ignores that the processes and procedures that neurodivergent employees need to have adapted were designed for a neurotypical workforce, a paradigm that we call the *Accommodations Dilemma*. Requiring employees to identify as disabled benefits those with severe needs while stigmatizing employees who have spent decades overcoming the challenges of workplaces designed for neurotypical workers. Employees who hide—or *mask*—their neurodivergence at work to avoid the professional and social costs attached to being considered "disabled" forgo accommodations at the expense of their own stress, mental exhaustion, and job performance.[6]

The current size of the neurodivergent population in the U.S. national security community is unknown. Within government disability data, government reporting does not distinguish different causes of disability, resulting in all disabilities being lumped together, such that employees with cognitive diagnoses are reported with amputees, deaf and vision-impaired employees, employees with psychological accommodations, and so on. As a result of this practice, along with the tendency for some employees to choose not to be categorized as disabled, the true size of the neurodivergent population employed in the national security

---

[5] Nicole Ogrysko, "Biden Calls for Agency Ideas to Win the Race for National Security Talent," *Federal News Network*, February 5, 2021.

[6] Masking is defined and explained in Chapter 3.

community is unknowable using the data and reporting methods in existence as of this writing. The resulting lack of data leads to two barriers to change: (1) Government officials described to us their assumption that neurodivergence is not prevalent in the national security workforce and (2) officials described their assumption that this lack of visible prevalence is not due to any systemic discrimination. Without understanding the size of the affected population, neither of these assumptions can be objectively examined.

Several aspects of the recruitment and hiring process can pose barriers to a neurodiverse workforce, including unclear or confusing job descriptions, complex application processes, job interviews that focus more on social and behavioral norms than on technical knowledge and skills, and lack of awareness by security clearance investigators. Within the military, barriers to entry include (1) unclear and unevenly applied requirements for recruits to prove that their diagnosis will not interfere with their service and (2) prohibitions on the use of prescribed medications, such as for ADD or ADHD.

Once on board, neurodivergent employees can face challenges navigating careers in workplaces that were not designed with them in mind. These challenges include sensory overload, rigid and tightly packed schedules, unspoken social mores, unclear career progression paths, and lack of clarity in instruction. Creating a supportive workplace will likely require some changes to workplace practices, such as onboarding, mentoring, and communications, along with an increase in awareness about what neurodiversity is and how it affects the workplace.

Recommendations

Government organizations that choose to embrace neurodiversity have many options. There are countless programmatic styles and philosophies from which to draw their organizational strategy. Some organizations have chosen to create pilot programs, others have developed enduring programs for neurodivergent workers, and still others have focused on embracing inclusivity and pivoting the entire organization to celebrate and embrace neurodiversity. We recommend the latter option, and we provide recommendations that include low-cost or no-cost solutions that could be implemented immediately, along with longer-term solutions that could lead to systemic change across the national security enterprise. A complete and more detailed list of the following recommendations is provided in Chapter 6:

- **Provide all employees equally with accommodations that mitigate the effects of sensory stimulation.** These accommodations might include (1) the ability to select one's desk location or to change or remove light bulbs to reduce brightness, (2) access to noise-canceling headphones, and (3) periods of minimal or no interruptions.
- **Modify job vacancies and hiring practices to attract neurodivergent candidates.** Changes to hiring practices could include using concrete, jargon-free language in job descriptions, eliminating unnecessary "requirements," and updating the interview process to align with practices from other organizations that recruit neurodivergent candidates.

- **Help all employees understand neurodiversity.** Opportunities to build understanding include inviting experts to present on the topic of neurodiversity, requiring empathy and psychological safety training for managers, and supporting agency affinity groups that are not tied to disability.
- **Support systemic change across the organization**. Organizations can also pursue broader systemic change. This might include incorporating neurodivergent people into major policy decisions, making changes to the security clearance process, examining military recruitment processes that can exclude qualified candidates, and revising policies that limit deployment and overseas travel for neurodivergent individuals.

This report provides research and analysis for national security leaders, managers, and employees who seek to better understand neurodivergence and neurodiversity and who desire simple and implementable steps to achieve neurodiverse inclusivity for their workplaces.

Contents

Boxes and Tables

Boxes

Tables

Chapter 1. Introduction

National security organizations need highly skilled and intellectually creative individuals who are eager to apply their talents to address the nation's most pressing challenges. In discussions—including during public sessions hosted by the Intelligence and National Security Alliance (INSA)—government and industry participants addressed the high stakes of the national security threats facing the United States; the demand for a STEM-skilled[7] and technology-savvy workforce; and the need to fill jobs that require enormous attention to detail, precision, and a low tolerance for errors.[8]

> "I played college ball, joined the military, joined my agency. I've worked as a polygrapher. I have autism."
>
> —Interview participant. This quote was edited to obscure the identity of the speaker. An explanation of our methods and use of quotes is provided later in this chapter.

In these discussions, participants addressed the need for *neurodiversity* in the national security community. They described missions that are too important and too difficult to be left to those who use their brains only in *typical* ways.

Neurodivergent is an umbrella term that covers a wide range of cognitive diagnoses,[9] including (but not exclusive to) autism spectrum disorder (ASD), attention deficit disorder (ADD) and attention-deficit/hyperactivity disorder (ADHD), dyslexia, dyscalculia, and Tourette's syndrome.[10] Neurodivergent individuals are already part of the national security

---

[7] STEM stands for science, technology, engineering, and mathematics.

[8] INSA, K2Workforce Neurodiversity NatSec Network Kick-Off Event, May 23, 2022; National Reconnaissance Office government official, interview with the authors, June 2, 2022; Office of the Director of National Intelligence government official, interview with the authors, June 14, 2022.

[9] *Neurodivergence* can apply to cognitive and/or developmental diagnoses. Because it is a nonmedical term and we were not conducting a medical research study, we do not intentionally exclude either group. *Developmental* diagnoses tend to focus on birth through adolescent development; because this study was exclusively focused on working-age adults, we chose to use *cognitive* throughout this report.

[10] This definition for neurodivergent was adapted from the Autistic Self Advocacy Network. There is no authoritative definition for *neurodivergence* or *neurodiversity*, so we use the following:

> Neurodiversity refers to variation in neurocognitive functioning. It is an umbrella term that encompasses neurocognitive differences such as autism, attention deficit hyperactivity disorder (ADHD), dyslexia, Tourette's syndrome, anxiety, obsessive-compulsive disorder, depression, intellectual disability and schizophrenia, as well as 'normal' neurocognitive functioning, or neurotypicality. Neurodivergent individuals are those whose brain functions differ from those who are neurologically typical, or neurotypical. (Employer Assistance and Resource Network on Disability Inclusion, "Neurodiversity in the Workplace," webpage, undated).

Some readers may prefer the term *neurodistinct*. At the time of this writing, neurodistinct was gaining popularity in the community because it eliminates the connotation of being *divergent from the norm* and replaces this with a positive connotation of being *distinct*. However, a decisive universal change in language has not occurred as of this writing; therefore, for this report, we use *neurodivergent*. We understand and respect that the language related to

workforce. They are serving as intelligence officers, engineers, security clearance investigators, military service members, and more. Some are senior managers, and it is likely that some are high-ranking executives. However, many of these individuals do not openly acknowledge their neurodivergence, for reasons that we will explain later in this report.

Many *neurotypical* people—people whose cognitive and mental processes are considered "typical" or "normal"—have preconceived, and often negative, notions about autism, Tourette's syndrome, dyslexia, and ADD/ADHD.[11] Other countries, such as Israel, the United Kingdom, and Australia, have established programs to ensure that *neurodiversity*—the full range of neurological types—is represented in their national security workforces.[12] Within the United States, some national security agencies have created small programs to onboard small numbers of neurodivergent employees.[13]

U.S. national security organizations, including intelligence organizations, the military services, and the Departments of Defense, State, and Homeland Security, face an ongoing recruitment and retention challenge.[14] These organizations need more people in general, and they need people who are able to meet specific capability requirements and who can fill gaps at specific locations and in specific job positions. National security organizations have also made commitments to building a diverse, equitable, and inclusive workforce, and these commitments currently fall short for their neurodivergent military and civilian workforces.[15]

Focus of This Study

The purpose of this study was to examine the following questions:

- What benefits (e.g., specific skills, aptitudes, advantages) do people with neurodivergence bring to national security organizations?

---

these topics evolves and can be controversial. We strove to select the most widely accepted terms and definitions at the time of publication, while realizing that language is fluid as society changes.

[11] Dawn Hendricks, "Employment and Adults with Autism Spectrum Disorders: Challenges and Strategies for Success," *Journal of Vocational Rehabilitation*, Vol. 32, No. 2, 2010; Alliyza Lim, Robyn L. Young, and Neil Brewer, "Autistic Adults May Be Erroneously Perceived as Deceptive and Lacking Credibility," *Journal of Autism and Developmental Disorders*, Vol. 52, No. 2, February 2022.

[12] Shira Rubin, "The Israeli Army Unit That Recruits Teens with Autism," *The Atlantic*, January 6, 2016; Robert D. Austin, Michael Fieldhouse, Aiyaswami Mohan, and Peter Quinn, "Why the Australian Defence Organization Is Recruiting Cyber Analysts on the Autism Spectrum," *Harvard Business Review*, December 7, 2017; Vincent Wood, "GCHQ Targeting Dyslexic and Neurodiverse People in Recruitment Drive, Spy Chief Says," *Independent*, October 21, 2019.

[13] See, for example, National Geospatial-Intelligence Agency, "NGA Launches Neurodiversity Pilot," press release, January 13, 2021.

[14] Nicole Ogrysko, "Biden Calls for Agency Ideas to Win the Race for National Security Talent," *Federal News Network*, February 5, 2021.

[15] Executive Order 13985, *Advancing Racial Equity and Support for Underserved Communities Through the Federal Government*, White House, January 20, 2021; Executive Order 14035, *Diversity, Equity, Inclusion, and Accessibility in the Federal Workforce*, White House, June 25, 2021.

- What are the challenges (e.g., limitations, team dynamics, and collaboration) in recruiting, working with, and managing a neurodiverse workforce?
- What barriers might exist in national security workplaces (e.g., in hiring, obtaining a security clearance, and onboarding; performance review processes; promotion and management; retention) that prevent agencies from realizing the benefits of neurodiversity?

Our goals were to (1) provide a compendium of publicly available literature, including scholarly literature, about neurodiversity in workforces, (2) relate that research to the national security community based on our combined experience with and understanding of the community, (3) conduct a series of discussions inside government and with key stakeholders to understand lessons learned and practices for the national security enterprise, and (4) provide a list of opportunities and recommendations for the government that is relevant across the range of national security missions and career fields.

In this report, we use the term *neurodiversity* to encompass all types of people: the full range of neurocognitive functioning, including both *neurotypical* and *neurodivergent* people. We refer to a specific cognitive difference, such as autism (or ASD) or dyslexia, only when the research we are citing is specific to one diagnosis. Therefore, *autistic* will be used only to refer to people on the autism spectrum when the discussion is specific to people with ASD.[16] In all generalizable cases, we will use *neurodivergent* to describe people who have any type of neurocognitive difference. We acknowledge that language associated with neurodiversity is fluid and evolving. We have selected to use the most widely accepted terminology in use at the time of this writing, knowing the risk that several of these terms may change, become outdated, or not be preferred by some readers.

In this report, we focus exclusively on neurodiversity and neurodivergence because we found these topics to be understudied in the community and widely ignored in government policies, practices, and procedures. Although we recognize that these diagnoses often exist concurrently (called *co-occurring*) with anxiety, depression, and other emotional and behavioral diagnoses, we do not focus on these co-occurring diagnoses because the national security community has policies and processes in place to address emotional and behavioral diagnoses.

Study Methods

Our study methods comprise three parts: literature review, interviews and discussions, and analysis.

---

[16] Language is important, and person-first language is a significant area of discussion in this community. Throughout the report, we choose to use the term *autistic person* rather than *person with autism* because some members of the community consider their autism to be a part of who they are rather than a disability that needs to be overcome. This perspective is not unanimous, and we understand that different readers may have different opinions (Mykola Bilokonsky, "How to Talk About Autism Respectfully," Public Neurodiversity Support Center, December 19, 2021).

Literature Review

The literature review included three types of literature: primary literature, secondary literature, and commercial literature. This section will describe each of the three types and the method and search criteria we used to search for relevant documents. After we began our analysis of literature, we conducted targeted searches to fill any gaps. Targeted searches included literature about polygraph exams and other topics that may include material that does not specifically reference neurotypes or diagnoses.

Primary literature consisted of scholarly and academic literature from the past ten years that was peer-reviewed. We began with 74 peer-reviewed articles as part of our initial literature review. We focused on research published within the five years before this study began (2016–2021) and referred to older research (2010–2016) only when it addressed topics that had not been further studied and reported. The majority of research on neurodivergence is focused on children, and only a small amount was relevant to graduating students entering a workforce or employees already in a workforce.

The second category in our literature review was *secondary literature,* or literature that drew on existing research to generate new conclusions. This secondary literature filled in gaps for populations for which primary research is not being conducted but findings can be drawn. It included articles written by advocacy organizations that represent neurodivergent job candidates and that help employers hire neurodivergent candidates, along with op-eds and first-person articles by experts and practitioners. This category included first-hand observations that are not captured in the other two categories.

The third category was *commercial literature,* which was both the most relevant to the national security community and the sparsest in citations, data, and methods. This category includes literature from companies depicting their internal programs and describing their lessons, practices, and performance measures but not providing their data or methodology. This category was most helpful in understanding practices that are transferrable to other large employers and knowledge organizations, such as the national security enterprise, but this literature was not peer-reviewed by any outside organization.

In conducting our literature searches, we used several methods and search terms. First, we began by searching Web of Science and Scopus for peer-reviewed publications and non–peer-reviewed publications that may be captured in these databases. Next, we used internet (Google) searches to seek secondary and commercial literature, including op-eds, commentaries, news publications, and blogs. The search terms we used included *autism spectrum disorder, attention-deficit/hyperactivity disorder, dyslexia, dyscalculia, Tourette's syndrome, neurodivergent, neurodiversity, neurocognitive functioning, workplace, workforce, work, college, graduate, employment, hiring, retention, recruitment,* and related workplace terms. For each of these terms, we included variations (e.g., *autism, autistic, autistics, Asperger, ASD*). Our initial search yielded 170 results, which we reviewed and then added to with targeted searches, as described above.

Interviews

After our literature review, we conducted a series of semistructured interviews and discussions with three populations: government officials, researchers or advocates who study or represent the interests of neurodivergent populations, and large organizations that have neurodiversity employment programs. Table 1.1 provides a list of the organizations we interviewed that agreed to be cited; this is not a complete list, as some nongovernmental interview participants asked that their organization be withheld.

Table 1.1. Selected Organizations in Interviews and Discussions

Government Interviews	Nongovernmental Interviews
• Department of the Air Force • Department of the Army • DoD Washington Headquarters Services • DoD Office of Diversity Management and Equal Opportunity • National Reconnaissance Office • Department of Homeland Security • Office of the Director of National Intelligence • Central Intelligence Agency • National Geospatial-Intelligence Agency (NGA)	• Ernst & Young (EY) • Google • Lawrence Fung, Stanford University • Alan Kriss, Specialisterne

NOTE: DoD = U.S. Department of Defense. This is not a complete list of all organizations that participated in this study.

The protocol we used when conducting these interviews is provided in Appendix A. Our goal was to capture organization-level and program-level practices, not to collect or report on the individual experiences of neurodivergent employees. To avoid asking an underrepresented and sometimes discriminated group to "out themselves," we did not ask any interview participants to identify themselves as neurodivergent. However, during the course of our interviews and discussions, several interview participants self-identified as such, and some government officials contacted us directly to ask to be interviewed. Throughout this report, we use quotes to represent the perspectives shared with us, and we have edited interview quotes to obscure the identity of the speaker.

Analysis

The third and final step in our methodology was analysis. We merged the findings from across our research to present a view of the complicated landscape for neurodiversity in large organizations in general and in national security specifically. The result of that analysis is presented in the following chapters.

- First, our analysis revealed a need for a *business case*, or a case for change. Although some readers may agree that promoting neurodiversity is the right thing to do, others may demand a more substantive, mission-driven reason. We address this in Chapter 2.
- Next, we found a paradigm that shapes this issue in the government. This paradigm—how the government approaches "accommodations"—sets the tone for the entire employer-employee relationship; we address this in Chapter 3 and offer alternatives.
- We found a variety of practices and lessons on attracting, hiring, and managing a neurodiverse workforce. We present these findings in Chapters 4 and 5, and we include a discussion of challenges and other findings that apply specifically to the national security community.
- In Chapter 6, we present a series of recommendations for U.S. government agencies to leverage internally. Our analysis also led to several conclusions on actions that have been effective in other organizations and/or that are likely to be effective in the government. We provide these for readers who may have the authority and ability to implement them.

Chapter 2. Why National Security Needs Neurodiversity

It is possible that the neurodivergent population in the national security workforce numbers in the tens of thousands, even though only small numbers of individuals openly reveal themselves as neurodivergent. Consider a simple calculation: Within the U.S. population, an estimated 5–20 percent of people are dyslexic,[17] 9.4 percent of children have been diagnosed with ADHD,[18] and more than 2 percent of the U.S. population is autistic.[19] As diagnostic assessment tools continue to proliferate to households that previously lacked access to such resources, these numbers may rise. DoD employs 1.3 million active-duty uniformed service members, nearly 900,000 civilians, and 1 million members of the ready reserve;[20] and the Departments of Homeland Security and State employ 240,000 and 24,000 employees, respectively.[21] Therefore, if a mere 1 percent of this population was neurodivergent, this group would number more than 34,000 people. Neurodiversity—the skills and qualities that employees across the full range of cognitive differences possess—can strengthen an organization, as many commercial firms discussed in this chapter have discovered.

In 1943, one of the first scientists to publish research on autism identified a group of highly intelligent children who could reproduce complex problems yet desired aloneness and sameness.[22] In 1944, one researcher described a mild-mannered, highly intelligent set of boys who struggled with social interactions.[23] In these early research studies, autism—as it later came

---

[17] Maria Cunningham, "Barriers to the Diagnosis of Dyslexia in Children," *Yale Undergraduate Research Journal*, Vol. 2, No. 1, Spring 2021.

[18] Diagnosis for all forms of neurodivergence often occurs during childhood, and children with these diagnoses will usually grow into adults with these diagnoses. Meanwhile, adults who fell through the cracks and were not diagnosed as children might not get diagnosed later in life, leading them to experience the challenges described in this report but without the knowledge of the cause for their struggles (Melissa L. Danielson, Rebecca H. Bitsko, Reem M. Ghandour, Joseph R. Holbrook, Michael D. Kogan, and Stephen J. Blumberg, "Prevalence of Parent-Reported ADHD Diagnosis and Associated Treatment Among U.S. Children and Adolescents, 2016," *Journal of Clinical Child & Adolescent Psychology*, Vol. 47, No. 2, March–April 2018).

[19] Centers for Disease Control and Prevention, "Data & Statistics on Autism Spectrum Disorder," webpage, last reviewed March 2, 2022a.

[20] DoD, Office of the Deputy Assistant Secretary of Defense for Military Community and Family Policy, *2020 Demographics: Profile of the Military Community*, 2021, p. 3.

[21] The State Department number does not include overseas locally employed staff (U.S. Department of Homeland Security, "About DHS," webpage, updated April 5, 2022; U.S. Department of State, "About the U.S. Department of State," webpage, undated.

[22] Steve Silberman, *NeuroTribes: The Legacy of Autism and the Future of Neurodiversity*, Avery, 2015.

[23] This condition later became known as Asperger's Syndrome, which is no longer diagnosed in the United States. In 2013, it became part of one umbrella diagnosis of ASD in the *Diagnostic and Statistical Manual of Mental Disorders*, Fifth Edition (Ruth I. Karpinski, Audrey M. Kinase Kolb, Nicole A. Tetreault, and Thomas B. Borowski,

to be called—was associated with high levels of intelligence. Today, ASD is medically defined as a "developmental disorder."[24] Studies have sought to measure the link between intelligence quotient (IQ) and ASD, and a 2018 study found that "there is a greater incidence of ASD in offspring whose parent(s) are in professions typically associated with a high cognitive ability, particularly those in engineering or the hard sciences."[25] This research aligns with the earliest autism research from the 1940s.[26]

Many neurodivergent people have skills that can fill the talent needs of the national security community. Laurent Mottron, a preeminent psychiatrist and autism researcher, notes that autistic people outperform neurotypical people in several skills, such as "spotting a pattern in a distracting environment," a skill that is likely particularly useful in intelligence or on a battlefield. Mottron attributes such skills as stemming, in part, from the fact that autistic brains "rely less on their verbal centres." He attributes this finding with the failure of employers to "realize what autistics are capable of" because "autistics tended to score much higher in the non-verbal [intelligence] test than in the verbal one . . . in some cases, as many as 90 percentile points higher."[27] As a result, hiring processes that rely on a verbal assessment—such as a verbal interview with a candidate—are focusing on the wrong factors, according to Mottron. In a series of experiments, researchers found that children with ASD outperformed neurotypical children in multiple tasks, including constructing and recognizing patterns.[28] In a study of neurodivergent and neurotypical individuals ages 14–36, researchers found that autistic individuals outperformed a neurotypical control group on a nonverbal intelligence test.[29]

To be clear, these findings do not present a holistic view of the entire neurodivergent population. But they demonstrate that many neurodivergent individuals possess skills that can help accomplish the missions of many national security organizations.

"High Intelligence: A Risk Factor for Psychological and Physiological Overexcitabilities," *Intelligence*, Vol. 66, January–February 2018).

[24] National Institute of Mental Health, "Autism Spectrum Disorder," webpage, undated.

[25] Karpinski et al., 2018. Notably, most of the research conducted on ASD and other cognitive differences was based on research studies composed entirely of Caucasian men. Therefore, researchers are only now beginning to learn how these conditions may present differently in girls and women and other races and ethnicities.

[26] Silberman, 2015.

[27] Laurent Mottron, "Changing Perceptions: The Power of Autism," *Nature*, Vol. 479, November 3, 2011, p. 34.

[28] Elizabeth Pellicano, Murray Maybery, Kevin Durkin, and Alana Maley, "Multiple Cognitive Capabilities/Deficits in Children with an Autism Spectrum Disorder: 'Weak' Central Coherence and Its Relationship to Theory of Mind and Executive Control," *Development and Psychopathology*, Vol. 18, No. 1, March 2006.

[29] Isabelle Soulières, Michelle Dawson, Fabienne Samson, Elise B. Barbeau, Chérif P. Sahyoun, Gary E. Strangman, Thomas A. Zeffiro, and Laurent Mottron, "Enhanced Visual Processing Contributes to Matrix Reasoning in Autism," *Human Brain Mapping*, Vol. 30, No. 12, December 2009.

Advantages of Neurodivergent Employees

Fundamental strengths that are common among the neurodivergent population can translate into job strengths, particularly in certain career fields of interest to national security. Autistic traits are also associated with an increased presence in careers related to computing, information technology (IT), engineering, and physics;[30] more-advanced digital skills;[31] up to 40 percent faster problem-solving;[32] and better systematizing skills.[33] Many neurodivergent individuals already in the workforce are aware of these strengths.

In interviews and surveys, neurodivergent software engineers have described themselves as being skilled at pattern recognition, visualization, and achieving a state of hyperfocus to complete a project.[34] In an interview with the American Bar Association's *Law Practice Magazine*, autistic lawyer Haley Moss spoke to her strength in reviewing documents, stating that she regularly notices details missed by others.[35] Air Force MSgt Shale Norwitz, who works on operational planning, said, "I'm on the [autism] spectrum and that makes me good at being a strategic thinker, and contributes to my innovation."[36] In an interview with *CBS This Morning*, Morgan McCardell, an intelligence analyst for NGA, described how her autism gives her an edge: "I can take what it would take a week for somebody (else) to do in a couple of hours."[37]

> "We need people who are detail-oriented, tech savvy, clearable, focused, diligent. Need ability to tag imagery of a Russian MIG-29 painted like a Ukrainian MIG and hidden in a jungle. When Tesla needs images of stop signs tagged, they send the imagery to China. We can't do that with national geospatial data."
>
> —CEO who hires autistic employees

These self-reported strengths are regularly echoed by the colleagues of workers with autism. In a focus group with the colleagues of trainees hired through an autism employment program,

---

[30] Simon Baron-Cohen, "Autism and the Technical Mind," *Scientific American*, Vol. 307, No. 5, November 2012.

[31] Katy-Louise Payne, Ailsa Russell, Richard Mills, Katie Maras, Dheeraj Rai, and Mark Brosnan, "Is There a Relationship Between Cyber-Dependent Crime, Autistic-Like Traits and Autism?" *Journal Of Autism And Developmental Disorders*, Vol. 49, No. 10, October 2019.

[32] Soulières et al., 2009.

[33] India Harvey, Samuela Bolgan, Daniel Mosca, Colin McLean, and Elena Rusconi, "Systemizers Are Better Code-Breakers: Self-Reported Systemizing Predicts Code-Breaking Performance in Expert Hackers and Naïve Participants," *Frontiers in Human Neuroscience*, Vol. 10, May 17, 2016.

[34] Meredith Ringel Morris, Andrew Begel, and Ben Wiedermann, "Understanding the Challenges Faced by Neurodiverse Software Engineering Employees: Towards a More Inclusive and Productive Technical Workforce," *Proceedings of ASSETS 2015*, October 2015.

[35] M. Suzanne Hartness and John D. Bowers, "Neurodiversity in the Practice of Law," *Law Practice Magazine*, November 1, 2020.

[36] Tre Davis, "Airman Advocates for Neurodiversity in Military," U.S. Air Force, August 6, 2021.

[37] "Autistic Analysts Help U.S. Spy Agency," *CBS This Morning*, April 21, 2022.

participants noted that the trainees produced high-quality work.[38] We heard from managers of an autistic employee that the organization has trouble keeping him assigned to projects because "we give him a month-long project to work on and he finishes it in two weeks."

Private-Sector Employers Seek Neurodivergent Candidates

Many employers—particularly those in need of highly skilled technical workers—have taken note of the capabilities possessed by neurodivergent individuals, and some have initiated programs to increase their hiring of neurodivergent employees. These programs are driven not by charity but by a desire to realize business gains from hiring talented employees. One leader at DXC, a technology company, said his efforts to start an autism hiring program "pushed it as a talent gain [and] didn't sell it as a disability program or some kind of inclusion initiative, but as capability uplift."[39] The *Autism @ Work Playbook*, a guide for employers developed by leaders from Microsoft, SAP, JPMorgan Chase, EY, and other organizations, describe such programs as a way to fill a need for skilled workers.[40]

STEM fields in particular are seeing increased demand for neurodivergent individuals. Jose Velasco, an executive at SAP and one of the authors of the *Autism @ Work Playbook*, emphasizes the value that some autistic individuals can add in STEM fields: "They have exceptional memory skills, and see patterns in systems and in data that others might not see."[41] Discussing workers in his lab who are autistic, Mottron notes, "None of my lab members is a savant. They are 'ordinary' autistics, who as a group, on average, often outperform non-autistics in a range of tasks, including measures of intelligence."[42] The chief executive officer (CEO) of Auticon, an IT consultancy that exclusively hires autistic people, is careful to avoid essentializing autistic people in describing his hiring strategy: "We don't want to give people the impression that all autistic people are IT geniuses, or that there are not neurotypical people who can do all of these things. But in the right role, and with the right support, an autistic person will significantly outperform a neurotypical person doing the same job."[43]

---

[38] Jennifer R. Spoor, Simon M. Bury, and Darren Hedley, "Non-Autistic Employees' Perspectives on the Implementation of an Autism Employment Programme," *Autism*, Vol. 25, No. 8, November 2021.

[39] Esther Shein, "Hiring from the Autism Spectrum," *Communications of the ACM*, Vol. 63, No. 6, June 2020, p. 17.

[40] H. Annabi, E. W. Crooks, N. Barnett, J. Guadagno, J. R. Mahoney, J. Michelle, A. Pacilio, H. Shukla, and J. Velasco, *Autism @ Work Playbook: Finding Talent and Creating Meaningful Employment Opportunities for People with Autism*, ACCESS-IT, The Information School, University of Washington, 2019.

[41] Ronnie Polaneczky, "A 'Rich Ecosystem of Support' for Adults with Autism Led to One Young Employee Filing Two Patents for SAP," *Philadelphia Inquirer*, November 13, 2019.

[42] Mottron, 2011, p. 33.

[43] Luke Mintz and Dominic Penna, "'Once I'm Focused on a Task, I Won't Stop': Why Employers Are Hiring More Autistic People," *The Telegraph*, January 28, 2020.

These hiring practices appear to be translating into business gains. Although concrete data from the commercial sector is hard to come by due to a lack of transparency about such programs, several companies are increasing the size of their neurodiversity programs, indicating that they have reaped value from these investments. EY—the accounting firm with $45.4 billion in annual revenue and operations in more than 150 countries[44]—started with one Neuro-Diverse Center of Excellence in 2016 and has since opened 13 other locations, with plans to keep expanding.[45] The CEO of SAP—a technology firm with annual revenue of €27 billion (approximately $29 billion)[46]—stated that teams that included an individual with ASD experienced "a rise in patent applications and innovations in products," among other benefits.[47] A representative of Siemens, one of Auticon's clients, said that Auticon's consultants increased their team's efficiency at product testing by 50 percent.[48] The founder of Autonomy Works, which monitors content on websites, said that autistic employees produced a 90 percent reduction in errors and a 30 percent increase in productivity.[49]

In one survey, employers reported that autistic employees outperformed their neurotypical colleagues in attention to detail.[50] In another study, interviewed managers highlighted the positive qualities of their employees with ASD, including having "vast knowledge" and "great talent" and being "very loyal" and "dependable."[51]

Many of these companies mention concrete goals related to hiring from neurodiverse groups. A Google executive described the company's interest in training "up to 500 Google Cloud managers and others who are involved in hiring processes" to work with autistic candidates and increase Google's hiring from this group.[52] EY's 14 Neuro-Diverse Centers of Excellence

---

[44] EY, "EY Achieves Highest Growth in Nearly Two Decades, Reports Record Global Revenue of US$45.4b," press release, September 21, 2022.

[45] Richard Tzul, "Growing EY Initiative Promotes Workplace Neurodiversity," Bloomberg Tax, June 13, 2022.

[46] SAP SE, *SAP Integrated Report 2021*, 2022.

[47] Carol A. Adams, "Neurodiversity at Work Benefits Everyone—Why Companies Are Hiring Autistic People," *The Conversation*, September 24, 2020.

[48] Hazel Davis, "Forget Stereotypes . . . How to Recruit Talented, Neurodiverse Employees," *The Guardian*, August 31, 2017.

[49] Anderson Cooper, "Recruiting for Talent on the Autism Spectrum," *60 Minutes*, July 18, 2021.

[50] Melissa Scott, Andrew Jacob, Delia Hendrie, Richard Parsons, Sonya Girdler, Torbjörn Falkmer, and Marita Falkmer, "Employers' Perception of the Costs and the Benefits of Hiring Individuals with Autism Spectrum Disorder in Open Employment in Australia," *PloS ONE*, Vol. 12, No. 5, May 18, 2017.

[51] Jessica Dreaver, Craig Thompson, Sonya Girdler, Margareta Adolfsson, Melissa H. Black, and Marita Falkmer, "Success Factors Enabling Employment for Adults on the Autism Spectrum from Employers' Perspective," *Journal of Autism and Developmental Disorders*, Vol. 50, No. 5, May 2020.

[52] Steven Aquino, "Google Cloud Exec Rob Enslin Talks Neurodiversity in the Workforce and How the Autism Career Program Seeks Top Talent," *Forbes*, July 26, 2021.

employ more than 300 people globally.[53] In 2014, SAP stated its goal to have 1 percent of its workforce composed of people with ASD.[54]

Benefits for a National Security Workforce

Several features of national security work overlap with the skill sets of many neurodivergent individuals, including the need to exert high levels of focus, remember highly detailed information, and perceive patterns in vast amounts of information. At an INSA event, one defense contractor's CEO described how his autistic workforce tags geospatial imagery with high precision rates and low error rates. He described NGA's need for a cleared contractor force to whom imagery could be outsourced for tagging, and he bragged that his employees could tell the difference between a Russian MIG, a Ukrainian MIG, and a Russian MIG painted like a Ukrainian MIG.

Sometimes, neurodivergent candidates and employees are motivated by different drivers than are typical or expected of employees. In some cases, these differences provide opportunities for national security employers in hiring and retaining this population. For example, some neurodivergent employees may be motivated only if a task is "intrinsically interesting," whereas other neurodivergent employees prefer repetition that requires deep concentration. National security agencies offer jobs that could appeal to both types of candidates, and these motivations align well with employers that are not offering the top salaries for such careers as cyber-related professions.

One experimental study found that, compared with non-autistic people, autistic people were more likely to behave ethically when not being observed. In this study, autistic people chose a morally good cause that inflicted a personal cost versus a morally bad cause that guaranteed a personal gain.[55] Autism is associated with rules-based behavior, which is well aligned with work in a classified environment.[56] Although a common stereotype we heard about was the false belief that autistic people cannot be trusted because they cannot understand the importance of rules, the opposite was more commonly described to us in interviews: Autistic people can thrive in environments with clear rules for accepted and unaccepted activities.

---

[53] Tzul, 2022.

[54] Shirley S. Wang, "How Autism Can Help You Land a Job," *Wall Street Journal*, March 27, 2014.

[55] Yang Hu, Alessandra M. Pereira, Xiaoxue Gao, Brunno M. Campos, Edmund Derrington, Brice Corgnet, Xiaolin Zhou, Fernando Cendes, and Jean-Claude Dreher, "Right Temporoparietal Junction Underlies Avoidance of Moral Transgression in Autism Spectrum Disorder," *Journal of Neuroscience*, Vol. 41, No. 8, February 24, 2021.

[56] Simon Baron-Cohen, Emma Ashwin, Chris Ashwin, Teresa Tavassoli, and Bhismadev Chakrabarti, "Talent in Autism: Hyper-Systemizing, Hyper-Attention to Detail and Sensory Hypersensitivity," *Philosophical Transactions of the Royal Society B: Biological Sciences*, Vol. 364, No. 1522, May 27, 2009; Simon Baron-Cohen, "The Hyper-Systemizing, Assortative Mating Theory of Autism," *Progress in Neuro-Psychopharmacology and Biological Psychiatry*, Vol. 30, No. 5, July 2006.

Much national security work, including intelligence analysis, requires keen attention to detail and the ability to excel while performing repetitive tasks in gathering and analyzing information. Employees with ASD may be more motivated by repetitive tasks, rather than seeking variety and autonomy in work.[57] In an experimental study comparing autistic and non-autistic individuals' performance on a visual search task, there was no difference in accuracy between the two groups in the first round; however, in the second round, the autistic group's performance improved, whereas the non-autistic group's performance diminished.[58] Interviewees reported that autistic employees improve their effectiveness with repetition, while neurotypical employees will demonstrate fatigue when conducting repetitive tasks, such as monitoring imagery for changes or examining large datasets for errors. A CEO of a defense contractor firm reported that a majority of his workforce has ASD and that these employees have a low error rate and a high tolerance for repetition when tagging geospatial intelligence imagery.

Some governments already benefit from the talents of their neurodivergent employees. In Israel, the Israeli Defense Force's Unit 9900 gathers, analyzes, and maps visual intelligence, such as satellite imagery, with the aid of "dozens" of autistic soldiers. In the future, autistic applicants will be able to train to serve in "quality assurance, programming, and information sorting."[59] Australia's Department of Defence is also building a neurodiversity program focused on cybersecurity,[60] and interview participants alluded to a similar program in the United Kingdom's national security community.

Neurodiversity Effects Across an Organization

Hiring a neurodiverse workforce can help fill high-skill roles that are challenging to hire for and can have broader positive effects across an organization. Christine Comaford, a leadership coach, noted that after EY started a pilot program to hire people with autism, its managers became more mindful and better communicators: "[T]he company's managers started to reflect more deeply and stretch to make sure they were communicating in a more effective manner."[61] Advocates at Microsoft also incorporated the positive impact on managers as part of their business case for expanding the company's Autism @ Work program.[62] Christian Klein, the

---

[57] Joanna Maria Szulc, Julie A. Davies, Michał T. Tomczak, and Frances-Louise McGregor, "AMO Perspectives on the Well-Being of Neurodivergent Human Capital," *Employee Relations*, Vol. 43, No. 4, 2021.

[58] Cleotilde Gonzalez, Jolie M. Martin, Nancy J. Minshew, and Marlene Behrmann, "Practice Makes Improvement: How Adults with Autism Out-Perform Others in a Naturalistic Visual Search Task," *Journal of Autism and Developmental Disorders*, Vol. 43, No. 10, October 2013.

[59] Rubin, 2016.

[60] Erica C. Collins and Emilee Schipske, "Global Neurodiversity: A Workplace Primer on Attracting and Retaining Neurodiverse Talent," *LaborSphere*, blog, July 26, 2021.

[61] Christine Comaford, "Is Neurodiversity the Right Talent Path for Your Organization?" *Forbes*, June 24, 2017.

[62] Annabi et al., 2019.

CEO of SAP, has said that teams with autistic colleagues experience "an increase in management skills and empathy."[63]

In the next three chapters, we will address achieving inclusivity of neurodiversity, as well as hiring and working with neurodivergent talent.

---

[63] Adams, 2020.

Chapter 3. Accommodating Differences While Valuing Inclusivity

Within the U.S. government, neurodivergent diagnoses are treated as a disability. During our research, as we engaged departments and agencies to interview government officials about the topic of neurodiversity, we were referred to the Equal Employment Opportunity (EEO) Office or the Office for Diversity, Equity, and Inclusion; in each office, we were referred to the professionals responsible for persons with disabilities. From the government perspective, as described to us in interviews, the appropriate venue for requesting an accommodation for an employee is to apply under an approved disability.[64] Any employee who does not have a recognized disability—that is, a disability recognized on Standard Form 256[65]—is expected to be able to interact with the same processes and procedures as the rest of the workforce. This policy position ignores the reality that those processes and procedures were designed for a neurotypical workforce and that they can serve as barriers to the hiring and retention of neurodivergent individuals.

None of the neurodivergent individuals we interviewed described themselves as disabled, and many were offended that they would have to be declared disabled for their employer to address the challenges they face in the workplace. Furthermore, the Schedule A letter

> "This letter serves as certification that (Name of individual) is a person with a severe disability that qualifies him/her for consideration under the Schedule A hiring authority."
>
> —Department of Labor Schedule A Letter

that an applicant or employee receives upon approval of their disability status declares that the employee "is a person with a *severe* disability" (emphasis added).[66] From the employee's perspective, a person who does not consider themself to be disabled may take offense that others—including their employer and supervisor—seem to work so hard to declare them disabled instead of providing a workplace that is inclusive of all cognitive types.

These include employees who have spent *decades* overcoming and managing their neurocognitive difference to succeed in a neurotypical world and who now have to declare themselves as "disabled" simply, for example, to have access to noise-canceling headphones in a bustling sensitive compartmented information facility (SCIF) environment. Although EEO officers sometimes describe policies, such as the ability to obtain a Schedule A letter, as a job protection and a ticket for accommodations, the employees we spoke with describe that same letter as a stigma and an insult to their dignity. As a result, many neurodivergent employees who

---

[64] U.S. Office of Personnel Management, "Reasonable Accommodation," webpage, undated.

[65] U.S. Office of Personnel Management, "Self-Identification of Disability," SF 256, revised October 2016.

[66] Department of Labor, "Schedule A Letter," undated.

are able to hide or downplay their neurodivergence may choose to do so, missing out on accommodations that could contribute to their success and that of their organization.

The dilemma that results from this policy paradigm is portrayed in the *Accommodations Dilemma* we developed (Box 3.1). The Accommodations Dilemma occurs when a person needs to be declared "disabled" in order to access accommodations that could instead reasonably be made available in their job. Such accommodations could include modifying department and agency policies and practices to allow employees to change their desk light bulb's brightness, use noise-canceling headphones in classified facilities, or request to switch desks with another peer on the team. Today's national security workplaces were designed by and for neurotypical workers, so such accommodations are considered deviations from the norm. Such accommodations could remove barriers to neurodiversity and inclusivity, yet none of these accommodations are the norm in any government office where we conducted our research. National security agencies regularly permit medical devices to be used in classified facilities, and military services provide eyeglasses to service members, but—without a declaration of disability—accommodations that would assist neurodivergent employees are not offered.

Box 3.1. The Accommodations Dilemma

The Accommodations Dilemma illustrates the deep-seated effects of the need for employees to request accommodations (and therefore declare themselves disabled) or else work within neurotypical processes (which one interview participant summed up as being told by a manager to "suck it up, buttercup").

If the Accommodations Dilemma extended beyond neurodiversity into gender diversity, the effects would resemble the historical scenario of inviting women to serve in the military and requiring them to wear the same "unisex" uniforms as the men.[a] Uniforms were historically designed by men for men, and although a woman is capable of wearing a man's clothes, shoes, and body armor, a uniform that was not designed for her will not fit properly, will restrict freedom of movement, may cause pain—such as in the case of body armor—and will impair her ability to thrive at her job. If, in this scenario, female service members needed to be declared "disabled" to request an accommodation of a gendered uniform, then such a process would create excess work, would require women to walk around with a visible appearance of being "othered" (by wearing something different than her "normal" fellow service members), and would create a feeling of not being included in the team and of having to hide her discomfort in order to "be one of the guys." In this scenario, a woman's inability to succeed in a unisex uniform is a disability in need of an accommodation, rather than a reflection of a male-oriented workplace that did not acknowledge its lack of gender inclusivity.

That said, neurodivergence is not as straightforward as a choice of uniforms. The range of diagnoses, and the range of ways that each diagnosis presents in individuals, creates a reality in which some people actually do identify as "severely disabled" (as described in Schedule A) and benefit from accommodations outside those that are reasonable for an entire workforce. In this regard, the relationship between neurodivergence and disability might be more analogous to the relationship between vision and disability than it is to gender. Vision challenges exist across a complex range of options. Some people need eyeglasses all the time, others just for reading, and some people have no eyesight at all. Some workers need assistive software on their computers, while others can magnify text using already installed tools. Some are colorblind, and others struggle with depth perception. In today's workplace, the needs of the job determine *which* vision challenges create a disability. A person who wears glasses or who is colorblind may be able to serve as a diplomat but not as a pilot. Therefore, the existence of a vision diagnosis and the need for eyeglasses or assistive tools is not automatically a disability; rather, such a distinction is made based on the needs of the job.

The Accommodations Dilemma occurs when a person needs to be declared "disabled" in order to access accommodations that could instead be made in consideration of the nuances of their needs and their job.

[a] Kimberly Curry Hall, Kirsten M. Keller, David Schulker, Sarah Weilant, Katherine L. Kidder, and Nelson Lim, *Improving Gender Diversity in the U.S. Coast Guard: Identifying Barriers to Female Retention*, Homeland Security Operational Analysis Center operated by the RAND Corporation, RR-2770-DHS, 2019; Agnes Gereben Schaefer, Jennie W. Wenger, Jennifer Kavanagh, Jonathan P. Wong, Gillian S. Oak, Thomas E. Trail, and Todd Nichols, *Implications of Integrating Women into the Marine Corps Infantry*, RAND Corporation, RR-1103-USMC, 2015; Mark D. Faram, "Sweeping Uniform Changes Emphasize Gender Neutrality," *Navy Times*, October 9, 2015.

Another challenge related to the classification of neurodivergence as a disability is that the federal government has difficulty gathering useful data on employees with disabilities. During our interviews, government employees explained that, when data are reported, all disabilities are lumped together, such that employees with cognitive diagnoses are reported with amputees, deaf and vision-impaired employees, employees with psychological accommodations, and so on. As a result of this practice, along with the tendency for employees to choose not to allow themselves to be categorized as disabled, the true size of the neurodivergent population employed in the national security community is unknown. In one DoD office, a person whose official job responsibilities include equal opportunity and diversity described the challenge as one of scale: If an agency's workforce is half women and half nonwhite racial minorities, then the EEO and diversity office is focused on supporting larger populations in the workforce and does not necessarily provide equal priority to a neurodivergent population that may be only a handful of employees. (Although these proportions are not accurate, this viewpoint represents the perception of one official we spoke with.)[67] This prioritization decision is based on two unfounded assumptions that were conveyed to us during interviews with government officials: (1) Neurodivergence is not prevalent in the national security workforce, and (2) the reason for this lack of visible prevalence is not due to discrimination. Without studies to examine either of these assumptions, government officials are making decisions based on unexamined assumptions.

> "If I could snap my fingers and be nonautistic, I would not—because then I wouldn't be me. Autism is part of who I am."
>
> —Temple Grandin, as quoted in Oliver Sacks, *An Anthropologist on Mars: Seven Paradoxical Tales*, Knopf, 1995, p. 292

The "Need" for Disclosure

If the number of neurodivergent employees in national security organizations is indeed so high, although only a small number of employees have revealed their status publicly, one might hypothesize that the neurodivergent population has already successfully integrated into the national security workforce. Some readers might consider this to be a sign of success: "Neurodivergent employees already work here! So, what's the problem?"

A handful of autistic members of the national security community whom we spoke with compared themselves with today's LGBTQ workforce. Both groups can hide in plain sight, choosing when and to whom to reveal themselves. Both groups include people for whom their label is a core attribute of their being, yet this same label can be a target of discrimination and harassment in the national security community. Two autistic intelligence officers said they are

---

[67] In reality, DoD reports that the department is 18.7 percent female and 29.8 percent nonwhite minorities. The generalization captured in the text reflects how that agency's EEO office makes decisions about prioritizing neurodiversity compared to other forms of diversity (DoD, 2021, pp. 6–7).

hoping neurodivergent national security professionals can eventually work openly and come "out of the closet" just as their LGBTQ colleagues have.

For some of these employees, neurodivergence is something they feel the need to hide or downplay at work, masking themselves to appear neurotypical for employers who do not know how to value the benefits of a cognitively diverse knowledge workforce or for coworkers who might harass and bully them, as some interviewees described. Without overcoming the data problem, the government has no means to measure and track the effects of neurodiversity on performance reviews, accessions, retention, and attrition and will not have documented motivation to address the disparities.

One challenge employers face in normalizing accommodations and hiring practices that benefit neurodivergent applicants is that providing these accommodations requires the neurodivergent individual to disclose their diagnosis to the employer. Job applicants' concerns that disclosure will lead to discrimination are not unfounded. One 2014 study, using over 6,000 fictitious cover letters, found that "experienced applicants with disabilities were 34 percent less likely to get responses than their nondisabled counterparts."[68]

Neurodivergent people have legitimate reasons not to disclose their diagnosis; without this disclosure, employers may not know that employees or applicants could benefit from accommodations. One government official said this difficulty with disclosure could harm otherwise qualified neurodivergent candidates, while noting that President Joe Biden's 2021 executive orders are improving cultural awareness of the need to provide accommodations.[69]

The Opposite of Accommodations

Perhaps the opposite of providing accommodations is *universal design*. When the enterprise is designed for everyone and accommodations are not needed—or are needed only for *severe* disabilities, as Schedule A describes—then perhaps neurodiversity can truly be attained.

The U.S. Department of Labor, citing the Americans with Disabilities Act, defines *accommodations* as "modification or adjustment to a job, the work environment, or the way things are usually done during the hiring process." The purpose of these accommodations is typically to provide equal opportunity to those who might otherwise not be able to secure or succeed in employment.[70] Employers are legally required to provide accommodations that would allow an employee to conduct their job; in some situations, this requirement leads to the question of why the job did not allow that change from the beginning.

---

[68] Dory Devlin-Rutgers, "Employers Show Bias Against People With Disabilities," *Futurity*, January 5, 2016; Mason Ameri, Lisa Schur, Meera Adya, F. Scott Bentley, Patrick McKay, and Douglas Kruse, "The Disability Employment Puzzle: A Field Experiment on Employer Hiring Behavior," *ILR Review*, Vol. 71, No. 2, March 2018.

[69] Executive Order 13985, 2021; Executive Order 14035, 2021.

[70] U.S. Department of Labor, Office of Disability Employment Policy, "Accommodations," webpage, undated.

In recent years, the diversity, equity, and inclusion community has been recommending a focus on the concept of *universal design* as an alternative to individual accommodations. The Centre of Excellence in Universal Design defines this concept as "the design and composition of an environment so that it can be accessed, understood and used to the greatest extent possible by all people regardless of their age, size, ability or disability."[71] This negates the need to make special accommodations for whole portions of users after the fact.

For example, the need for software that magnifies or dictates writing for employees who are vision or hearing impaired and ramps for employees who use wheelchairs or canes are typical accommodations found in most modern workplaces. These same accommodations can benefit *all* employees. Ramps are useful for workers pushing heavy carts and for visitors with baby strollers. Magnification and text-to-voice are common features in most business software. Ergonomic workspaces, according to the U.S. Department of Labor, can be thought of as "productivity enhancers."[72] Simple adjustments, such as providing private workspaces, job expectations in writing,[73] and noise-canceling headphones,[74] would benefit many other employees as well as neurodivergent employees.

When employers offer accommodations that require a disclosure of disability, requesting these accommodations can entail a social cost for employees. In a study, managers were more willing to approve accommodations from employees with a demonstrated history of strong performance,[75] even though another study found that the colleagues of disabled workers considered accommodations for workers who were already performing well to be unfair.[76] At the same time, research shows that managers sometimes have lower expectations for workers with ASD and other disorders.[77] Outing oneself as neurodivergent opens a worker up to judgment from colleagues: Research shows—and interview participants revealed—a fear that requesting

---

[71] Centre for Excellence in Universal Design, "What Is Universal Design," webpage, undated.

[72] U.S. Department of Labor, Office of Disability Employment Policy, undated.

[73] Morris, Begel, and Wiedermann, 2015.

[74] Jennifer Lewington, "In the Global Hunt for Tech-Savvy Workers, Companies Are Turning to a Once-Ignored Source of Talent: Those Diagnosed with Autism," *Globe and Mail*, February 25, 2021.

[75] Anna T. Florey and David A. Harrison, "Responses to Informal Accommodation Requests from Employees with Disabilities: Multistudy Evidence on Willingness to Comply," *Academy of Management Journal*, Vol. 43, No. 2, April 2000.

[76] Ramona L. Paetzold, María Fernanda Garcia, Adrienne Colella, Lily Run Ren, María del Carmen Triana, and Monique Ziebro, "Perceptions of People with Disabilities: When Is Accommodation Fair?" *Basic and Applied Social Psychology*, Vol. 30, 2008; Toschia M. Hogan and Joseph Liu, "Status Is the Difference: Disability and the Unintended Consequences of Fairness," *Academy of Management Proceedings*, Vol. 2018, No. 1, 2018.

[77] Lily Run Ren, Ramona L. Paetzold, and Adrienne Colella, "A Meta-Analysis of Experimental Studies on the Effects of Disability on Human Resource Judgments," *Human Resource Management Review*, Vol. 18, No. 3, September 2008.

accommodations may make employees targets for discrimination.[78] Government contractors face similar concerns: Although they know that their employer is bound by federal rules, including the Americans with Disabilities Act, they also fear that asking for one of the accommodations described above would label them as unfit for the customer's worksite and therefore unemployable in a SCIF.

Research conducted during the coronavirus disease 2019 (COVID-19) pandemic found that, as workers return to the office, some enterprises "were not built for or with disabled people in mind" and that "in order to truly promote DEI [diversity, equity, and inclusion], it is necessary to embrace intersectionality and support people's whole identities including their disabilities."[79]

Perhaps the opposite of requiring employees to declare themselves disabled in order to access accommodations is to *not require* them to declare themselves by making these benefits available to everyone.

Accommodating Neurodiversity

For employees who are neurodivergent, the list of accommodations—or workplace changes—that could be helpful includes technology tools, process changes, and training for their supervisors, their colleagues, and themselves. Employers may choose to think about accommodations as workplace changes to enhance hiring, onboarding, and workplace practices for all, rather than as tailored solutions that apply only to a specific set of people who have requested them and been deemed eligible to receive them.

Some examples of discrete accommodations suggested during our interviews included technological solutions, such as memory aids and dictation software that translates speech into text, and coaches or accommodations officers who help the employee and agency navigate which accommodations might be beneficial even in restrictive workplace environments. One official discussed the difficulty of implementing technological accommodations, noting that the security features of government computer systems often present the greatest hurdle to the use of such solutions. At Microsoft, employees with ASD or ADHD described accommodations they needed when navigating team dinners, receiving instructions only verbally, attending frequent meetings, and working in an open floor plan office space.[80]

Neurodivergent government employees must thus choose between requesting an accommodation and facing the potential for discrimination resulting from this choice or forgoing any sort of accommodation and potentially having their personal stress levels (and job

---

[78] Emma Day-Duro, Grace Brown, and Julian Thompson, *Thinking Differently: Neurodiversity in the Workplace*, HULT International Business School, undated.

[79] Kaela S. Singleton, De-Shaine R. K. Murray, Angeline J. Dukes, and Lietsel N. S. Richardson, "A Year in Review: Are Diversity, Equity, and Inclusion Initiatives Fixing Systemic Barriers?" *NeuroView*, Vol. 109, No. 21, November 3, 2021.

[80] Morris, Begel, and Wiedermann, 2015.

performance) suffer as a result. For example, an employee with noise, light, or smell sensitivity might benefit from having noise-canceling headphones, a desk far away from the SCIF door (which slams open and shut every few minutes), an environment free from heavy fragrances, removal of bright overhead lighting, etc. Should the employee need to be declared "disabled" to request these accommodations, which a neurotypical employee might consider "conveniences"? The difference, according to our interview subjects, is that a neurotypical employee might be mildly inconvenienced by this work environment, whereas a neurodivergent employee will find their work and concentration totally derailed for the day. The result could be that—because of environmental factors that could have been mitigated—the neurodivergent employee is considered unproductive and ineffective, leading to long-term effects on their performance, promotion potential, and ability to contribute to the mission.

In the next chapter, we offer a way to think about accommodations during the hiring process that benefit all applicants, not just neurodivergent ones. One private-sector executive we interviewed described requests for accommodations as a "broken" part of the hiring process, and the result is that neurodivergent candidates are left out of the conversations that will ultimately affect them. This executive recommended that, if an organization wishes to hire neurodivergent individuals at scale, it should seek to reform all its hiring processes to be broadly inclusive, rather than creating a dedicated pipeline to hire neurodivergent candidates.

Chapter 4. Recruiting Neurodivergent Talent for National Security

What does a neurodivergent-friendly recruitment process look like? In this chapter, we describe barriers and opportunities that can arise during the recruitment and hiring process. According to our research, the key to hiring neurodivergent talent is to ensure that the process does not get in the way of the desired outcome: to attract and recruit a highly skilled, diverse workforce. This means that it is necessary to revise or eliminate features of traditional job descriptions, interviews, and other parts of the process that do not address the actual requirements of the job or a candidate's qualifications to do the job but that nonetheless can pose barriers to hiring for neurodivergent individuals.[81]

During an interview with our team, one executive at a nonprofit that helps companies hire neurodivergent workers emphasized that there is no ready-made set of policies that a company can implement that will solve its neurodiversity problem. But the executive did offer advice to *remove the barriers* that stop neurodivergent candidates from applying to jobs and receiving offers. These barriers include unnecessary job "requirements" that are not truly needed for the job, such as requiring a degree instead of describing the knowledge or skills that are necessary. This executive also recommended (1) training managers to recognize and work with different people and (2) including skills assessments as part of the interview process. In this executive's view, an organization's ultimate goal should be to progress beyond the need for a dedicated program to hire neurodivergent workers and instead to implement changes to its fundamental hiring, onboarding, and management practices to be more inclusive of neurodivergence.

An organization seeking to increase the neurodiversity of its workforce will choose whether the end goal is to create a recruitment, hiring, and employment program *specifically for neurodivergence* or to create an inclusive workplace where neurodiversity is addressed across *all* recruitment, hiring, and employment programs. Some interview participants described this as the difference between creating a side entrance for neurodivergent candidates versus simply welcoming all candidates through the front door. Special job descriptions, interview protocols,

> "I find that when people say they want to hire people who think 'outside of the box,' they really mean people who think in a slightly larger box."
>
> —Interview participant

---

[81] Extensive research literature indicates that the most frequently used approaches for writing job descriptions and conducting candidate interviews are not actually effective tools for matching skills and ability to the needs of a position. We are aware of this body of literature but focus in this report on how these commonly used practices disadvantage neurodivergent candidates in additional manners. Readers interested in this topic should see Ann Marie Ryan and Robert E. Ployhart, "A Century of Selection," *Annual Review of Psychology*, Vol. 65, January 2014; and Sheldon Zedeck, ed., *APA Handbook of Industrial and Organizational Psychology:* Vol. 2, *Selecting and Developing Members for the Organization*, American Psychological Association, 2011.

and other practices just for neurodivergent candidates—though labeled as "accommodations"—are, even if unconsciously, creating an artificial "otherness" for neurodivergent employees. If full neuro-inclusivity is the end goal, employers will learn from their neurodivergent employees and can aim instead to provide universally inclusive employment practices that apply to everyone.

This chapter addresses research about attracting neurodivergent candidates, revising traditional interview processes to accommodate neurodiversity, engaging with third-party organizations to aid in recruitment and hiring, and considering issues that are specific to the military services.

Attracting Neurodivergent Candidates

One of the first barriers a neurodivergent job candidate might encounter is the job posting itself. Unclear or confusing job descriptions, or postings that include qualifications that are not really necessary to perform the job, can cause neurodivergent candidates to self-select out of the application process. Summarizing findings from interviews of university students and graduates on the autism spectrum, Jonathan Vincent notes that "the lack of clarity in job adverts was identified as being especially problematic."[82]

Before applying for a position, an applicant must make sense of government job postings, which is difficult enough for neurotypical applicants. A propensity for some neurodivergent people to think in literal terms adds to that difficulty: "If the job posting requires a certain number of years of cyber security experience, does my part-time job during college count? And, if so, how do I measure my work experience for a job that was not full-time?" or "The position requires 'strong communication skills'; what does that *literally* mean?" and so on through the list of potential landmines.

Having hired about 50 neurodivergent employees from 2016 to 2021, Toronto-Dominion (TD) Bank attracts neurodivergent applicants by writing clearer and more-straightforward job descriptions. These descriptions do not change the nature of the position being filled, yet they avoid excessive jargon and acronyms that create a barrier to understanding the role. For example, one of the company's job postings stated that the role would require the employee to align their work with an established standard. The original job posting phrased this requirement as "ensure the execution of your function is in line with documented procedures." The updated language asks the applicant a direct, concrete question that is both more informative and more appealing: "Does working with database systems to investigate and resolve errors to assure process accuracy and efficiency sound like something you would enjoy?"[83]

---

[82] Jonathan Vincent, "Employability for UK University Students and Graduates on the Autism Spectrum: Mobilities and Materialities," *Scandinavian Journal of Disability Research*, Vol. 22, No. 1, 2020.

[83] Lewington, 2021.

Table 4.1 shows examples of actual phrasing from government job postings and suggests edits that may more successfully attract neurodivergent candidates. We offer these suggested revisions based on literature and practices for attracting neurodivergent talent and based on the lessons described by experts in our interviews.

Table 4.1. Writing Effective Job Descriptions

Position Title	Traditional Phrasing	Neurodivergence-Friendly Phrasing
Contracting Officer Representative	*Serves as liaison* between contractors and the government contracting officer *to identify and resolve issues.*	Identifies, documents, communicates, and negotiates points of agreement and disagreement between contractors and the government contracting officer. Works with parties to resolve differences and identify solutions.
Cyber Operations Analyst	*Prepares oral and written correspondence and other documentation.*	Explains ongoing cyber operations to military leaders who do not have cyber expertise. Explains the significance of new cyber threats in terms of how previously unknown vulnerabilities are being exploited by adversaries. Documents results for use by future analysts.
Accountant	Minimum qualifications: *Demonstrated excellent:* • *Interpersonal skills* • *Verbal and written communication skills* • *Customer service* • Analytic and problem-solving abilities • Team and independent work ethic What You'll Need to Apply: • . . . A cover letter specifying your qualifications.	[Delete italicized section. Instead, replace it with a practical exercise. Three business days before the interview, provide the candidate with fake financial data and request that the candidate conduct an accounting analysis and present their findings to the interview committee. Evaluate the candidate on technical accuracy of the analysis and ability to effectively communicate key findings.]
Data Modeler	*Must possess clear, concise, and effective verbal and written communication, including the ability to effectively communicate with technical personnel, business customers, and management, and proven ability to think conceptually and abstractly.*	Ability to communicate your knowledge of complicated technical data in such a way that those in any nontechnical data roles will also be able to understand.

SOURCES: USA Jobs, "Contracting Officer Representative, Department of Defense, Missile Defense Agency," Announcement No. MDA-21-11170262-DH-OC, Control No. 608656900, accessed June 22, 2022a; USA Jobs, "Program Analyst (Cyber Operations), Department of the Air Force, Air Combat Command," Announcement No. s-22-DHA-11223362-JLE, Control No. 616240500, accessed June 22, 2022b; Central Intelligence Agency, "Accountant," webpage, undated; USA Jobs, "Business Analyst (Data Modeler/Metadata Specialist/Open Government Data Specialist), Federal Reserve System," Announcement No. DEST-11485818-22-CB, Control No. 652648400, accessed July 15, 2022c; Ronald Van Loon, "How to Become a Data Modeler in 2023?" Simplilearn, updated January 31, 2023.
NOTE: Emphasis added.

Candidates applying for national security positions must fill out a stream of forms, instructions, and questionnaires, which are written using neurotypical interpretations of language and which can be lengthy and confusing to a person with executive functioning challenges.[84] We heard multiple examples of candidates who began the paperwork process of applying and gave up simply because the process was overwhelming and confusing. Candidates who effectively navigate the application process report an entirely new set of challenges when they reach the security form SF-86, as described in Box 4.1.

Researchers have documented difficulties that neurodivergent individuals have when trying to complete forms;[85] anecdotally, we heard applicants describe their own difficulties. Autistic applicants described struggling to understand the "true meaning" of questions, which might have hidden implications or imprecise bounds, and both autistic and ADD/ADHD applicants described feeling overwhelmed by the amount of pages and sheer number of questions laid out in front of the applicant. Providing alternatives with fewer pages and fields to fill out could attract talented pools of potential workers whose brains function differently.

---

[84] *Executive function* is "the group of complex mental processes and cognitive abilities (such as working memory, impulse inhibition, and reasoning) that control the skills (such as organizing tasks, remembering details, managing time, and solving problems) required for goal-directed behavior" (Merriam-Webster, "Executive Function," webpage, undated).

[85] Day-Duro, Brown, and Thompson, undated.

Box 4.1. Navigating the Security Clearance Process

The security clearance process is an obstacle course of monumental proportions for candidates with poor executive functioning, atypical verbal communication, irregular or atypical body movements, sensory sensitivities, and other common attributes of neurodivergence: Sit still, don't fidget. Make eye contact, but not too much eye contact that you look suspicious. Answer questions promptly when asked, but do not sound rehearsed. Do not search too long for your answers. Do not question the foundation of the question or "split hairs." Understand the nature of the question, not its purely literal interpretation.

Some interview participants—including people who assisted job candidates in applying for national security jobs—described the sheer amount of paperwork alone as a seemingly insurmountable hurdle for applicants who struggle with executive functioning. An overwhelming effort can be required to recall every address where a person has lived for the past ten years and to fill out 100 percent of the fields on a security form *completely* before the form can be submitted. For candidates who understand language literally and struggle with nuance, the requirement to document every close foreign contact can feel like navigating a minefield. Their thoughts may look something like this: "The neighbor in the apartment across the hallway is friendly to me when we see each other; he has an accent; he is close in proximity and foreign, but if I do not know his full name, can I not apply for this job?"

> "People have looked right at me and said, 'No one with autism could work here, they couldn't pass the security clearance process.' They didn't know I am autistic."
>
> —Interview participant

For such a candidate, during an interview, answering the seemingly straightforward question "Have you ever betrayed someone close to you?" poses another obstacle. Imagine thinking, "I'm sure I've betrayed *someone* at *some point*, but I don't know who or when, so how do I answer this question? Let me think—which example should I use, or should I lie and say I never have simply because I can't think of an example?" This candidate might be face to face with an interviewer, unable to answer this question, and such a nonverbal response, along with a confused facial expression, could erroneously be interpreted as a sign that the person is trying to manufacture a lie and cannot be trusted.

Although a diagnosis of a *psychological condition*, as some types of neurodivergence are sometimes considered, cannot automatically disqualify a person from gaining clearance, the reality is much more complex and nuanced. Take the likely routine situation of a candidate who answers "no" to the question, "Do you have a mental health or other health condition that substantially adversely affects your judgment, reliability, or trustworthiness even if you are not experiencing such symptoms today?" When an applicant answers no to this question, and no relevant concerns arise during the investigation, then it is likely that investigators conducting their interview or polygraph are unaware of why the candidate's verbal response, body language, and/or eye contact is not within the range of what the examiner is trained to consider "normal." In these scenarios, interview participants—including a former polygraph examiner—said they worried about how many candidates do not pass the process because their behavior is considered "suspicious and untrustworthy" simply because it does not fall within the range of expected behavior.

People with autism or other neurodivergent diagnoses begin to learn *masking* at a young age. Masking is the ability to engage in a behavior that does not come naturally but that can be learned, even if doing so is uncomfortable. For example, an autistic person described to us that being forced to make eye contact is akin to staring directly into the sun: It can be done but is very uncomfortable. Adults who have successfully learned to mask their neurodivergent behaviors with more-neurotypical behaviors can find these skills highly useful in a workplace and a liability in the security clearance process. Is the polygraph subject who is making unblinking eye contact trying to hide a lie, or are they masking and unaware of the difference between neurotypical ("natural") eye contact and learned or forced ("unnatural") eye contact? Is the anomalous reading on the polygraph caused by differences in physiological responses in the skin of neurodivergent applicants? Is the person who is fidgeting in front of the investigator nervously hiding a counterintelligence threat, or are they using fidgeting to direct energy that would otherwise be spent rocking and swaying their body? Adults who have masked for decades in order to succeed in school and employment described to us not being able to "turn off" these behaviors because they have become so deeply ingrained.

According to a former polygraph examiner who identifies as autistic, the answers to such questions are unknown because security clearance investigators and polygraph examiners are not taught how neurodivergent applicants present differently. According to this official, this topic has never been studied.

SOURCE: Features information from William Henderson, "Mental Health and Final Security Clearances," ClearanceJobs, March 29, 2022.

Some interview participants questioned how a candidate might fare differently during the security clearance process based on whether they are neurotypical or are neurodivergent but not declaring their diagnosis. A 2022 study attempted to put empirical evidence against the question of whether autistic adults are perceived as being more deceptive or less credible. Thirty autistic and 29 neurotypical individuals participated in video-recorded interviews, and 1,410 people viewed one video each to rate their perception of the deception and credibility of the person being interviewed. The study "revealed that autistic individuals were rated higher on perceived deception and lower on perceived competence and character compared to neurotypical individuals."[86] Some of the reasons the raters provided for their assessment included gaze aversion, repetitive body movements, smiling/smirking/laughing, and inconsistent demeanor, along with a variety of other reasons. Interestingly, when the study participants were informed that the interviewed person may have an ASD diagnosis, there was no longer a significant measurable perception of deception, though a perception of lack of competence remained.[87]

A 1972 study is still used by some polygraph examiners today, and it teaches the idea of a "silent answer test," in which the subject being polygraphed is told not to answer any questions out loud but to only think about the answer in his head. The theory of this research is that a person will have internal conflict—he wants to lie, but there is no audible way to do so—and this internal conflict will appear on the device.[88] The study refers to all test subjects as "he" because women were not included, and our literature review revealed no indication that the research has been repeated with cognitive type as a variable (nor race, ethnicity, sexual orientation, or any other variable). In other words, people whose internal monologue differs from what was normal for men in 1972 may or may not be considered in today's polygraph techniques. Therefore, a polygraph subject who struggles to interpret the meaning of a question and struggles to form a response to a question may present differently than the standard that examiners were trained for, regardless of whether that person is hiding a lie.

The challenge this research presents for neurodivergent candidates applying to national security jobs is summed up in the Accommodations Dilemma: They can declare their diagnosis and benefit from accommodations in the security clearance investigation and hiring process, only to then face a bias of being perceived as less competent once they arrive on the job.

Revising the Traditional Job Interview

Traditional approaches to job interviews can eliminate neurodivergent candidates who are otherwise a strong fit for a position. Research has found that autistic job candidates are less

---

[86] Lim, Young, and Brewer, 2022, pp. 496–498.

[87] Lim, Young, and Brewer, 2022.

[88] Frank S. Horvath and John E. Reid, "The Polygraph Silent Answer Test," *Journal of Criminal Law, Criminology, and Police Science*, Vol. 63, No. 2, June 1972.

likely to be hired because of interviewers' lack of knowledge about autistic traits—such as concrete thinking, increased processing time, and sensory sensitivities, as well as reduced facial expressions, rapport, and reciprocation to smiles and handshakes—which can alter their impressions of the candidates.[89]

In one study, researchers found that, during traditional interviews, autistic applicants faced challenges caused by "literal interpretation of interview questions or audio distractions."[90] In another study, researchers performed an experiment in which autistic and non-autistic individuals took part in two mock interviews. After the first interview, the interviewers assessed the interviewee while the interviewees provided feedback on how the interview questions might be improved. The authors found that, in both interviews, autistic interviewees were assessed unfavorably relative to the non-autistic group. Both groups improved in the second interview, with the autistic group improving substantially more, indicating that practice improves the performance for autistic interviewees.[91] Some employers have internalized this lesson by giving applicants the interview questions in writing in advance, so applicants can be prepared and know they will not be surprised. Other employers describe conducting initial non-interview discussions to allow the candidate to build comfort with the process.

Other options are available to facilitate the hiring of neurodivergent candidates, and many of these practices can be applied across *all* candidates, regardless of cognitive type. Options include eliminating interviews altogether or making a dramatic shift from a traditional interview approach to an approach for screening candidates that involves practical skills, or *acuity assessments*.

A Google Cloud executive who is autistic suggested that many autistic candidates would more effectively pass through the hiring process if they were offered longer interview times or were allowed to answer questions in writing rather than verbally. Part of Google Cloud's

---

[89] Anna Melissa Romualdez, Zachary Walker, and Anna Remington, "Autistic Adults' Experiences of Diagnostic Disclosure in the Workplace: Decision-Making and Factors Associated with Outcomes," *Autism & Developmental Language Impairments*, Vol. 6, 2021; Camilla M. McMahon, Stacey Henry, and Meghan Linthicum, "Employability in Autism Spectrum Disorder (ASD): Job Candidate's Diagnostic Disclosure and ASD Characteristics and Employer's ASD Knowledge and Social Desirability," *Journal of Experimental Psychology: Applied*, Vol. 27, No. 1, March 2021; Mirah J. Dow, Brady D. Lund, and William K. Douthit, "Investigating the Link Between Unemployment and Disability: Lexically Ambiguous Words and Fixed Formulaic Sequences in Job Ads for Academic Reference Librarians," *International Journal of Information, Diversity, & Inclusion*, Vol. 4, No. 1, 2020; Katie Maras, Sue Mulcahy, Laura Crane, Tamsyn Hawken, and Amina Memon, "Obtaining Best Evidence from the Autistic Interviewee: Police-Reported Challenges, Legal Requirements and Psychological Research-Based Recommendations," *Investigative Interviewing: Research and Practice*, Vol. 9, No. 1, 2018; Katie Maras, Jade Eloise Norris, Jemma Nicholson, Brett Heasman, Anna Remington, and Laura Crane, "Ameliorating the Disadvantage for Autistic Job Seekers: An Initial Evaluation of Adapted Employment Interview Questions," *Autism*, Vol. 25, No. 4, May 2021.

[90] Anna Julian and Ronda Barron, "Employees with Asperger's Syndrome and Their Experiences Within the Work Environment," *DBS Business Review*, Vol. 3, 2019.

[91] Maras, Norris, et al., 2021.

solution to this problem has been to train staff who are involved with hiring to work appropriately with candidates on the autism spectrum.[92]

The common theme of such efforts is to *keep the assessment process focused on the nature of the job itself*, rather than on a candidate's ability to quickly build rapport with a stranger or the ability to fit in at a business dinner. Candidates distinguish themselves by demonstrating capacity or competence at the tasks they will be required to perform on the job, rather than through the traditional markers of work experience and skill at interviewing.

An executive at one global company told our team that they have eliminated interviews when screening candidates for the company's autism hiring program. The traditional interview process has been replaced with the following steps, which include an informal practical skills assessment:

1. The company conducts a "getting to know you" phone call with the candidate. The goal of this conversation is to allow the candidate to feel comfortable interacting with a member of the company. (The company strives to put "zero pressure" on the candidate during this call.) The discussion focuses on getting to know who the candidate is, and the conversation lasts at least one hour. The company's representative explains the hiring process to the candidate in as much detail as the candidate wants so there are no surprises later. The purpose of this discussion is to make the candidate feel comfortable, to demystify the hiring process, and to reduce the candidate's anxiety about the process.
2. Next, the company emails the candidate a practical exercise using Microsoft Office software (such as an Excel file filled with data). The candidate is given a set of instructions on how to analyze the data, and they are asked to provide their analysis and results back at any time that is convenient for them. No deadline is provided. The candidate is allowed to follow up with as many questions as they want. The company intentionally omits some instructions from the exercise in order to assess how well the candidate can accomplish a task with missing information. The candidate is assessed on their results, the creativity they demonstrate in their approach, and their technical strength.
3. After the exercise is returned, the company conducts a video conference call with the candidate. Cameras are optional during this discussion. This is the first "interview," but no typical interview questions are asked. The candidate presents their finished analysis of the Excel data, and the hiring officers ask questions as though they are the client receiving this presentation. They evaluate the candidate on analytic skills and ability to conduct the task at the level of quality expected. They observe the candidate's ability to interact with a team while responding to technical questions that challenge their work. Traditional interview questions are not used.

An Australian psychotherapist who specializes in helping patients with ASD, ADD/ADHD, and other diagnoses provided the following list of suggestions for employers:

- Offer a pre-interview visit to the place where the candidate will be interviewed.

---

[92] Aquino, 2021.

- Inform the interviewee of what is going to happen and what is expected of them ahead of time.
- Provide the interview questions in advance.
- Minimize interruptions and avoid unnecessary "waiting room" time (the latter of which can be extremely anxiety-provoking for an autistic person).
- Adapt the environment for potential sensory issues, such as a flickering light.
- Adapt language to the interviewee.
- Replace ambiguous, open-ended questions, such as "tell me about yourself," with questions that require specific details, examples, and certain types of information.
- If a question has more than one part, ask each part in turn.
- Provide a printout of the questions so the interviewee can refer to them during the interview and stay on track.[93]

At EY, the hiring process for neurodivergent workers includes exercises that test applicants' skills and ability to work on a team. Applicants are given direct feedback on their performance over the course of the engagement.[94] EY organizes these hiring efforts through its Neuro-Diverse Centers of Excellence, including hiring on the autism spectrum. The company's first Neuro-Diverse Center of Excellence also included hires with ADHD and dyslexia.[95]

From 2015 to 2019, Microsoft hired more than 100 people on the autism spectrum. Like EY, Microsoft has a dedicated program for hiring neurodivergent candidates. Microsoft's Director of Inclusive Hiring and Accessibility Neil Barnett said that the process for hiring autistic workers extends over five days (compared with one day for the company's typical assessment process).[96] He said roughly half of the autistic employees hired through this program had previously applied to Microsoft but failed to receive an offer: "We realized candidates with autism don't get through the initial phone screen because they may have yes or no answers or they may not elaborate on other skills."[97] Some of the accommodations Microsoft offers to circumvent this problem include offering practice interviews or skipping the phone screening altogether.[98]

In a bid to reach its goal to have neurodivergent people make up 1 percent of its total workforce, Goldman Sachs initiated an internship program targeted to the neurodivergent.[99]

---

[93] Adapted from Katie Maras, "What to Do When Interviewing an Autistic Person for a Job?" University of Bath, undated.

[94] Nara Schoenberg, "'We Don't Care About the Eye Contact.' Autistic People Thrive in Chicago Tech Jobs After Years of Underemployment," *Chicago Tribune*, June 11, 2019.

[95] EY, "EY US Launches First Neuro-Diverse Center of Excellence in Boston," press release, April 12, 2021.

[96] Naomi Rovnick, "Hiring More 'Neurodiverse' Workers Can Pay Dividends," *Financial Times*, November 20, 2019.

[97] Rovnick, 2019.

[98] Maitane Sardon, "How Microsoft Tapped the Autism Community for Talent," *Wall Street Journal*, October 26, 2019.

[99] Julia Horowitz, "Goldman Sachs Plans to Hire More Neurodiverse Employees, Including People on the Autism Spectrum," *CNN Business*, April 2, 2019.

Although applicants are hired into an internship, the program is geared toward long-term employment. The company states on its website that successful interns will be made an offer for a full-time job. All interns in the initial 2020 cohort were made an offer to continue working with the company.[100]

Revising the interview process—or doing away with it altogether—could help employers fill roles with talented neurodivergent staff. Government agencies may have latitude to make some useful changes in their hiring processes, in terms of how resumes are reviewed, whether cover letters are required, whether or how interviews are conducted, and other assessment tools. One government official told us that their agency has flexibility in how the specific hiring process is undertaken, as long as the process is consistent for all candidates. For example, the agency can forgo the interview stage of the process altogether, but it cannot selectively exempt certain candidates from interviewing. Therefore, changes to the hiring process, such as replacing a traditional interview with a practical exercise, could be evenly applied to all candidates for a single vacancy. Such an approach would institutionalize the universal design approach to creating inclusivity in neurodiversity.

Engaging with Third-Party Organizations

When beginning to implement a hiring process for neurodiversity, many organizations consult with a service provider that specializes in helping employers hire neurodivergent candidates. These providers include both nonprofit and for-profit organizations that work with employers to write job descriptions, develop interview or hiring protocols, and screen candidates, while sometimes coaching the candidates through the process to facilitate the best possible outcome for both parties. One reason to work with a third party is that there is no simple set of policies an employer can implement that will automatically correct its hiring practices. Professionals who are trained and experienced in spotting and overcoming difficulties can help avoid common missteps. One such expert said, "The specific supports and training will differ among companies and neurodivergent workers, but without them, individual placements often will not be successful for either the worker or employer."[101]

One way to think about these groups is as expert matchmakers. They work directly with hiring organizations to find, select, and train potential hires. In some cases, these assessors work directly with a client company to find candidates to fill a specific need. One such person described her goals in hiring neurodivergent individuals as follows: "I want to see how they work together and their technical skills."[102]

---

[100] Goldman Sachs, "Neurodiversity Hiring Initiative," webpage, undated.

[101] Michael Bernick, "Is Your Company Inclusive of Neurodivergent Employees?" *Harvard Business Review*, February 16, 2022.

[102] Wang, 2014.

When partnering with the MITRE Corporation on a Neurodiverse Federal Workforce pilot, a social service provider handled all of the initial candidate search, conducting resume reviews and phone screens, then collaborated closely with the participating government agency to find candidates with the right skill set and to host a weeklong skill-building and assessment seminar. After receiving training on how to equitably evaluate autistic candidates in the agency-required interviews, agency staff interviewed the candidates and selected pilot participants.

Arguably, the most critical role filled by third-party service providers is that of educator. If an organization is not adequately prepared to understand and support neurodivergent employees, recruiting and hiring efforts are a waste of money, and current neurodivergent employees are at higher risk of burnout. Professionally provided education can help managers, coworkers, and subordinates of neurodivergent employees recognize the strengths that neurodiversity brings to their team and can help them learn to communicate effectively so that everyone feels psychologically safe to bring all of their strengths to their team.

Working with a third party to stand up and support special programming can be an important first step to overcoming practices that are not neuro-inclusive in an organization, but it should not be the end goal. In our assessment, the long-term goal in any specially focused inclusion program should be to eventually not need that program.

Recruiting and Retaining Military Service Members

Military service members who are neurodivergent can face additional challenges. The U.S. military does not automatically disqualify candidates from active duty who disclose one of the diagnoses addressed in this report. Each military service has its own policy, and all services allow recruits to prove that their diagnosis will not interfere with their ability to serve.[103] However, strict policies can make it difficult to qualify. For example, according to the U.S. Naval Academy, "Academic skills defects, such as learning disabilities or Attention Deficit Hyperactivity Disorder are not disqualifying if academic success can be demonstrated without the use of classroom accommodations, and no medication has been used in the past 12 months, with good grades," meaning applicants must be able to mask their neurodivergence without medication.[104] Even with an excellent academic record, some applicants are turned away when they disclose their neurodivergence, as was the case for a student who had his Naval Reserve Officers' Training Corps (ROTC) scholarship rescinded when his autism diagnosis became known.[105]

---

[103] Rob Vrabel, "Can You Join the Military with Autism?" Operation Military Kids, June 7, 2021.

[104] U.S. Naval Academy, "Appendix A: Medical Considerations for Admissions," undated.

[105] Marcella Robertson, "Navy Rescinds Student's ROTC Scholarship Because of His Autism Diagnosis," *WUSA*, June 18, 2021.

During interviews with our team, service members who effectively manage their ADD or ADHD using prescription medications said they were told to choose whether to abstain from using treatments that have been effective for them or be declared "not deployable" because of their use of a daily medication. Interview subjects at the Central Intelligence Agency reported similar challenges but were unwilling to provide specific examples because of uncertainty about which agency policies are classified. In an era in which U.S. children with ADD or ADHD are likely to be medicated and the military services are facing critical recruitment shortfalls, these policies have direct effects on military recruitment and readiness.[106]

Although some service members shared their experiences with their own diagnoses, others shared the pitfalls involved in getting diagnosed or disclosing a diagnosis, saying that it might be better not to know during one's military career. One person wrote, "I'll get tested after I retire. Not worth losing my wings over, unfortunately."[107] Another person said, "Some of us are diagnosed. The military just dosen't [sic] know it. I was told by my recruiter not to mention it at MEPS [Military Entrance Processing Station]."[108] The perception here is that the military would rather turn a blind eye to neurodiversity than truly understand and embrace it. One person wrote, "The nuclear Navy would fail if we had comprehensive autism testing in the accessions pipeline."[109]

Ironically, anecdotal evidence suggests that neurodivergent soldiers thrive in military service. According to a 2022 article that included interviews with an autistic marine and the parent of an Army guardsman,

> Military life tends to agree with autistic people, who are typically focused and hardworking, said Arzu Forough, the president and CEO of Washington Autism Alliance. Her late son, Darian, was autistic and served in the Army National Guard, she told Stars and Stripes by phone Thursday.
>
> "The structure of military life—the predictability and the fact that expectations are very clear—is a really, really good thing for a person on the spectrum," she said. "They thrive in that type of structure. The more predictable things are, the better they thrive."
>
> The military also provides an autistic person with camaraderie and social support, Forough said.

---

[106] One study found that 62 percent of children ages 2–17 with ADHD were medicated. Data were not available for ADD (Danielson et al., 2018).

[107] NotchbackFiero, "I'll get tested after I retire. Not worth losing my wings over, unfortunately," Twitter post, June 24, 2022.

[108] Papasmurf811, "Some of us are diagnosed. The military just dosen't know it. I was told by my recruiter not to mention it at MEPS." Twitter post, June 23, 2022.

[109] J. C. Lundberg [@jclundberg], "The nuclear Navy would fail if we had comprehensive autism testing in the accessions pipeline," Twitter post, June 23, 2022.

Martinez said that becoming a Marine profoundly changed his life, especially his ability to communicate and pick up on social cues.[110]

Other neurodivergent service members shared their anecdotal experiences through social media. Writing on Twitter, self-identified service members said, "It's pretty much common knowledge in a lot of technical military MOS's [Military Occupational Specialties] that a bunch of our peers have undiagnosed ADHD or Autism,"[111] "I was diagnosed with ADHD as a FGO [field grade officer],"[112] and "I excelled as both an Apache crew chief and an EOD [Explosive Ordnance Disposal] tech[nician] . . . Add to that my ability to hyper-focus. EOD is the perfect job for someone with ADHD."[113]

If the military were to treat cognitive diagnoses as a spectrum—comparable to how it treats eyesight and vision diagnoses—then a diagnosis of neurodivergence or the need for a prescription might not require a waiver to serve, just as the need for eyeglasses does not require a waiver. In such a scenario, the services would assess the degree to which different cognitive diagnoses impair or impede military service, rather than placing the responsibility for *disproving* such impairment on the 18-year-old recruit.

---

[110] Kelly Agee and Alex Wilson, "Disabled People Fight US Military Disqualifications to Fulfill Their 'Duty to Serve,'" *Stars and Stripes*, April 21, 2022.

[111] LethalityJane, "It's pretty much common knowledge in a lot of technical military MOS's that a bunch of our peers have undiagnosed ADHD or Autism," Twitter post, June 23, 2022.

[112] powerswf, "I was diagnosed with ADHD as a FGO; prior enlisted SIGINT/Russian linguist. The military thrives because of us with ADHD. It's asinine to think they are screening people because of it. The only reason I got in is because us Gen-Xers never went to the doctor pre-military," Twitter post, June 23, 2022.

[113] WildAlaskanRed, "Add me to the list. I excelled as both an Apache crew chief and an EOD tech. The technical skill required was easy. The Army gave me structure so I didn't realize I had problems until I left," Twitter post, June 24, 2022a; WildAlaskanRed, "Add to that my ability to hyper-focus. EOD is the perfect job for someone with ADHD," Twitter post, June 24, 2022b.

Chapter 5. How to Work Successfully with a Neurodiverse Team

Neurodivergent employees face several challenges when navigating careers in workplaces that are not designed with them in mind. Challenges can include sensory overload, rigid time schedules, unspoken social mores, unclear career progression paths, and lack of clarity in instruction. Increasing the neurodiversity of an organization's workforce will thus likely require some changes to workplace practices. However, such accommodations do not need to be a burden: Organizations and leaders can create onboarding processes that benefit all employees and improve workplace communications in a manner that supports the diversity of the entire organization. Such steps could help both neurodivergent and neurotypical employees succeed and can create a more inclusive workplace. This chapter provides an overview of our research about onboarding employees and preparing the workplace, communicating across neurodiverse teams, and the value of supervisor training and other practices.

Onboarding and Preparing the Workplace

Building a neurodiverse workforce involves more than simply hiring neurodivergent workers. After hiring a new worker, an organization's next step is to guide them through an onboarding process that helps new hires get acclimated to the workplace and learn how to succeed there.

A successful onboarding experience can encourage new employees to stay with their employer longer. Research indicates that employees who went through a "structured onboarding program" were 69 percent more likely to remain with the company three years after starting than those who had not gone through such a program.[114] This is in line with advice from an executive coach: "New hires, in partnership with their manager, should identify 7–10 people—superiors, peers, direct reports, and internal and external customers—whose success they will contribute to, or who will contribute to their success."[115]

Although some literature on onboarding neurodivergent workers centers on the types of accommodations that employers can provide to their neurodivergent employees, several commercial organizations have taken a different approach, focusing on the onboarding experience, mentoring, and knowledge-sharing.

Potentia, an intermediary organization that helps employers hire neurodivergent workers, concentrates much of its effort on tasks beyond simply getting workers into a role. The

---

[114] Guangrong Dai and Kenneth P. De Meuse, "A Review of Onboarding Literature," Lominger Limited, January 12, 2007, p. 9.

[115] Ron Carucci, "To Retain New Hires, Spend More Time Onboarding Them," *Harvard Business Review*, December 3, 2018.

organization provides training for managers, arranges for mentorship opportunities, and helps the neurodivergent hire build an interpersonal support structure outside the office.[116] Google Cloud executive Rob Enslin has similar ambitions for his organization, with a focus

> to train up to 500 Google Cloud managers and others who are involved in hiring processes. Our goal is to empower these Googlers to work effectively and empathetically with autistic candidates and ensure Google's onboarding processes are accessible and equitable.[117]

Evidence suggests that training, mentorship, and technological solutions can help onboard new employees successfully, similar to how such activities have assisted students who are transitioning into college life.[118] Professor Lawrence Fung, the director of the Stanford Neurodiversity Project, has found that timing is an important factor in helping neurodivergent individuals succeed in the workplace. In a 2021 interview, he said, "Often these accommodations come way too late. They should be put in place day one of employment, so the employee doesn't have to ask for changes after things aren't working out." In the employment program Fung initiated at Stanford, both autistic employees and their employers receive support for 12 weeks after the hiring date.[119] This practice is similar to the one used by Specialisterne, which provides a coach for each neurodivergent consultant it places with an employer.[120]

Communicating in a Neurodiverse Workplace

In terms of workplace challenges, researchers cite literature showing that social and communication challenges pose particularly difficult barriers to the work success of autistic individuals.[121] These barriers are not one-way. Emerging research, in what Damian Milton calls the "double empathy problem," suggests that people on the autism spectrum communicate quite

---

[116] Bernick, 2022.

[117] Aquino, 2021.

[118] Emily Hotez, Christina Shane-Simpson, Rita Obeid, Danielle DeNigris, Michael Siller, Corinna Costikas, Jonathan Pickens, Anthony Massa, Michael Giannola, Joanne D'Onofrio, and Kristen Gillespie-Lynch, "Designing a Summer Transition Program for Incoming and Current College Students on the Autism Spectrum: A Participatory Approach," *Frontiers in Psychology*, Vol. 9, February 13, 2018.

[119] Tracie White, "Stanford Program Matches Autistic Job Seekers with Employers," Stanford Medicine, November 5, 2021.

[120] Gareth Cook, "The Autism Advantage," *New York Times Magazine*, November 29, 2012.

[121] Hendricks, 2010; Phame M. Camarena and Pamela A. Sarigiani, "Postsecondary Educational Aspirations of High-Functioning Adolescents with Autism Spectrum Disorders and Their Parents," *Focus on Autism and Other Developmental Disabilities*, Vol. 24, No. 2, June 2009; Eve Müller, Adriana Schuler, Barbara A. Burton, and Gregory B. Yates, "Meeting the Vocational Support Needs of Individuals with Asperger Syndrome and Other Autism Spectrum Disabilities," *Journal of Vocational Rehabilitation*, Vol. 18, No. 3, 2003; Michael B. Ruef and Ann P. Turnbull, "The Perspectives of Individuals with Cognitive Disabilities and/or Autism on Their Lives and Their Problem Behavior," *Research and Practice for Persons with Severe Disabilities*, Vol. 27, No. 2, June 2002; Laurie A. Sperry and Gary B. Mesibov, "Perceptions of Social Challenges of Adults with Autism Spectrum Disorder," *Autism*, Vol. 9, No. 4, October 2005.

well with one another.[122] Problems tend to escalate when communication involves both neurotypicals and autistic individuals.

Stereotypes that neurodivergent employees must be poor communicators can be misplaced and misinformed. Neurodivergent people can be highly effective communicators, such as actor Anthony Hopkins, New York assemblywoman Yuh-Line Niou, and Swedish climate activist Greta Thunberg, all of whom report being autistic.[123]

Neurodivergent people might communicate differently from neurotypical people and from each other,[124] and they may describe having difficulty navigating social interactions,[125] which is a challenge that would extend into workplace interactions. Workplace communication includes verbal, written, and nonverbal methods (including body language, facial expressions, and other types); it also includes manager-employee communication (communicating down), employee-manager communication (communicating up), and team communication or communication across departments (lateral communication). Each of these types of communication poses a different challenge to the most skilled neurotypical communicator and may present invisible challenges that neurotypical colleagues are not aware of.

During researchers' interviews with autistic employees about their experiences at work, employees shared examples of needing to rehearse what to say to avoid being too blunt in interviews, struggling to read people's faces, or interpreting and answering others' questions literally.[126] The challenge of literal interpretation was also noted by researchers studying autism, who described literal interpretation of questions as a particular challenge during job interviews.[127]

Just as neurodivergent workers may struggle with some forms of communication required in the workplace, neurotypical staff can also misinterpret signals they receive from neurodivergent colleagues. In interviews with our team, government employees described neurodivergent employees who are equally as mission-driven as their neurotypical peers, while researchers have reported that autistic workers tend to be less motivated by money and less focused on managing

---

[122] Damian E. M. Milton, "On the Ontological Status of Autism: The 'Double Empathy Problem,'" *Disability & Society*, Vol. 27, No. 6, October 2012.

[123] Zack Budryk, "More Celebrities Are Coming Out as Autistic. That Makes a Huge Difference," *Washington Post*, September 8, 2021.

[124] Day-Duro, Brown, and Thompson, undated; Centers for Disease Control and Prevention, "Signs and Symptoms of Autism Spectrum Disorder," webpage, March 28, 2022b.

[125] Emmanuelle Walkowiak, "Neurodiversity of the Workforce and Digital Transformation: The Case of Inclusion of Autistic Workers at the Workplace," *Technological Forecasting and Social Change*, Vol. 168, July 2021.

[126] Karen Hurlbutt and Lynne Chalmers, "Employment and Adults With Asperger Syndrome," *Focus on Autism and Other Developmental Disabilities*, Vol. 19, No. 4, Winter 2004.

[127] Julian and Barron, 2019.

the way they are perceived by others,[128] which can lead to them being perceived as "disengaged and unmotivated."[129] An autistic engineer, describing her beliefs about how colleagues interpret her behaviors, said, "My hesitation on acting on vague instructions portrays me as disinterested, lazy, and arrogant."[130]

To help remedy communication challenges, Auticon, an IT consulting firm that hires autistic consultants, hires coaches for its consultants. These coaches provide guidance to help autistic consultants avoid "anxiety or sensory overload." This guidance includes help with prioritizing their work tasks and encouraging consultants to take vacations.[131] Auticon also sends its coaches to the client site to train neurotypical coworkers on working with the neurodivergent consultants.[132]

Employers can use technological solutions to tailor communication styles to the intended recipient of a message. Although all individuals differ, there is substantial research examining the communications preferences of people with ASD. Summarizing interviews with 27 autistic students who had recently transitioned to college, researchers noted that the group universally expressed a preference for written communication (email) over speaking on the phone.[133]

To facilitate communication for employees who seek written options, researchers found that moving communication online when possible, through chat functions, forums, and similar tools, effectively enhances communication in the workplace.[134] Technological solutions need not be cutting-edge or expensive to be effective. In one set of expert interviews, an interviewee shared that an autistic worker would "signal [colleagues] if he was focused or approachable with coloured flags."[135] Another author described how color-coded indicators on conference badges "enabled Autistics to communicate their needs and desires without having to articulate them in

---

128 Ashley A. Scott-Van Zeeland, Mirella Dapretto, Dara G. Ghahremani, Russell A. Poldrack, and Susan Y. Bookheimer, "Reward Processing in Autism," *Autism Research*, Vol. 3, No. 2, April 2010; Coralie Chevallier, Gregor Kohls, Vanessa Troiani, Edward S. Brodkin, and Robert T. Schultz, "The Social Motivation Theory of Autism," *Trends in Cognitive Sciences*, Vol. 16, No. 4, April 2012.

129 Eric Patton, "Autism, Attributions and Accommodations: Overcoming Barriers and Integrating a Neurodiverse Workforce," *Personnel Review*, Vol. 48, No. 4, 2019; Szulc et al., 2021.

130 Anonymous, "A Visible Career on the Spectrum," *Chemical Engineer*, February 27, 2020.

131 Hazel Davis, 2017.

132 Adam Gale, "Why Linklaters Is Hiring Neurodiverse People," Management Today, updated September 24, 2020.

133 Charlotte Y. Alverson, Lauren E. Lindstrom, and Kara A. Hirano, "High School to College: Transition Experiences of Young Adults with Autism," *Focus on Autism and Other Developmental Disabilities*, Vol. 34, No. 1, March 2019.

134 Szulc et al., 2021.

135 Walkowiak, 2021, p. 7.

the pressure of the moment." In this example, each color was defined in advance, so the person using and reading the badge color did not need to decide nor ask what each color indicated.[136]

Many of these tools, such as instant messaging and email, already exist in workplaces. In those cases, the task of an organization's leaders may not be to implement new technological solutions but rather to encourage employees to be mindful of taking advantage of these technologies when possible. Other approaches, such as asynchronous collaboration via shared documents in the cloud, may already be implemented in many workplaces—not to promote neurodiversity, but as a response to the COVID-19 pandemic.[137] Employers can take this as an opportunity to study what works and what challenges remain. It may be that collaborating virtually rather than in-person, or emphasizing asynchronous written communication versus holding meetings, provides unexpected benefits. Or it could be the case that remote work creates challenges that will ultimately need to be surmounted to promote neurodiversity in the workplace. In any case, these changes provide an opportunity for organizations that are willing to learn and adapt.

Creating a Supportive Workplace

The Achievers Workforce Institute *2022 Engagement and Retention Report* found that 66 percent of employees surveyed reported that they planned to job hunt in 2022. As the United States as a whole struggles to find and retain talent, the Achievers study found that the "key to retention is having a strong culture of belonging."[138] That is no less true for retaining neurodivergent employees, who often provide support to one another. One private-sector executive we interviewed described the importance of affinity groups in the workplace. These groups, which the interviewee described as "support groups," can be organized around any number of topics, including religious identity, hobbies, and neurodivergence. Groups that focus

---

[136] Silberman (2015, p. 443) describes these badges and their meanings as follows:

> Even highly verbal autistic adults occasionally struggle with processing and producing speech, particularly in the chaotic and generally overwhelming atmosphere of a conference. By providing attendees with name-tag holders and pieces of paper that were red on one side and yellow on the other, they enabled Autistics to communicate their needs and desires without having to articulate them in the pressure of the moment. The red side facing out signified, "Nobody should try to interact with me," while the yellow side meant, "Only people I already know should interact with me, not strangers." (Green badges were added later to signify, "I want to interact but am having trouble initiating, so please initiate an interaction with me.") These color-coded "interaction signal badges" turned out to be so useful that they have since been widely adopted at autistic-run events all over the world, and name-tag labels similar to Autreat ("autistic retreat") green badges have recently been employed at conferences for Perl programmers to indicate that the wearer is open to spontaneous social approaches.

[137] Samuel, Alexandra, "As Remote Work Becomes the Norm, Vast New Possibilities Open for Autistic People," *Wall Street Journal*, March 8, 2021.

[138] Achievers Workforce Institute, *2022 Engagement and Retention Report: The Great Resignation Continues as Employees Seek Growth, Balance, and Support*, 2022.

on neurodivergence can emphasize professional development, bringing in outside experts as speakers; they can be purely social and plan fun group-selected activities, such as game nights; they can be a conduit for raising issues faced by neurodivergent employees to leadership and working to make systemic changes; or these groups might combine all three emphases.

Although affinity groups can provide support for neurodivergent employees, they are not sufficient in themselves to create a supportive workplace. Employers should also train neurotypical workers to understand the "needs and behaviors" of neurodivergent colleagues.[139] This includes understanding how behaviors on the part of neurotypical employees can have detrimental effects on neurodivergent employees. For example, in a 2013 study, researchers studied the effect of what they called *transformational leadership behaviors*—including the use of emotional language to motivate employees[140]—on the anxiety level and commitment to work of workers with ASD. The authors found that the use of emotional language to inspire workers actually *increased* the anxiety level of autistic employees.[141]

Increasing neurodiversity can be seen as a learning opportunity for managers. In a 2020 article about Australian managers of autistic employees, the authors reported that managers felt that support for autistic workers was not enough: The managers themselves needed support from "autism-specific or general disability vocational support providers."[142] After EY initiated its autism hiring program, managers worked to improve their own communication skills.[143] Several neurodivergent technology workers discussed the requests they had made (or would like to make) of their managers, including an employee with ADHD requesting permission to record meetings to avoid having to listen and take notes at the same time. Two interviewees mentioned that they would prefer to receive their manager's instructions and expectations in writing, yet one also said that he did not make this request of his manager because he did not want to disclose his ADHD diagnosis out of fear of consequences.[144]

In interviews with government officials and leaders in the private sector, many respondents emphasized the role of training for managers in achieving positive outcomes for employees, including neurodivergent employees. One government official emphasized the need for

---

[139] Michał T. Tomczak, "Employees with Autism Spectrum Disorders in the Digitized Work Environment: Perspectives for the Future," *Journal of Disability Policy Studies*, Vol. 31, No. 4, March 2021, p. 201.

[140] Examples of transformational leadership emotional language that were cited in this study include a manager who "says things that make employees proud to be a part of this organization," "says positive things about the work unit," and "encourages people to see changing environments as situations full of opportunities" (Alannah E. Rafferty and Mark A Griffin, "Dimensions of Transformational Leadership: Conceptual and Empirical Extensions," *Leadership Quarterly*, Vol. 15, No. 3, June 2004, p. 339).

[141] Alissa D. Parr, Samuel T. Hunter, and Gina Scott Ligon, "Questioning Universal Applicability of Transformational Leadership: Examining Employees with Autism Spectrum Disorder," *Leadership Quarterly*, Vol. 24, No. 4, August 2013.

[142] Dreaver et al., 2020, p. 1661.

[143] Comaford, 2017.

[144] Morris, Begel, and Wiedermann, 2015.

education regarding the capabilities of disabled people: promoting the understanding that, with accommodations, they can successfully accomplish their missions. An interviewee in the private sector discussed training hiring managers to at least recognize job candidates with autism and direct them to the company's dedicated program for hiring autistic individuals. A government official we spoke with commented on the need for their organization to train managers in how to work with neurodivergent individuals. This official described training and education for hiring managers as a way to help neurodivergent people broadly, including those who do not disclose a diagnosis, because those managers will be able to better interpret the communication they receive from all individuals.

Many approaches that would improve communication for neurodivergent employees could benefit the entire team, including many neurotypical employees. The array of potential solutions that might create successful workplace environments for neurodivergent workers is broad. In an article summarizing research on autism and employment, Hendricks groups recommendations from the literature into five categories: "(1) job placement, (2) supervisors and co-workers, (3) on-the-job provisions, (4) workplace modifications, and (5) long-term support."[145]

The literature provides other suggestions for supporting neurodiversity in the workplace. One segment of the academic literature shares the perspectives of neurotypical colleagues of neurodivergent workers. In a 2021 study, Spoor, Bury, and Hedley conducted focus groups with 32 colleagues of autistic trainees hired through an employment program for workers on the autism spectrum. These colleagues generally noted that developing greater knowledge about autism was helpful in their interactions with the autistic trainees.[146]

In a 2016 study, researchers conducted interviews with five individuals who worked at an organization providing job placement, coaching, and training services to clients with ASD. Several themes emerged from these interviews that shed light on how an organization might work successfully with colleagues with ASD. These themes include suggestions that managers of autistic employees should be knowledgeable about ASD, flexible in their management style, and accommodating of autistic employees' special needs. According to the researchers, interviewees also suggested that communicating with autistic colleagues in a direct manner and providing ongoing direct support would be useful accommodations to make.[147] Not coincidentally, direct communication and available direct support can be universally beneficial to the entire workforce.

In a series of interviews with the managers of people with autism, researchers reported that managers sought to find a balance between providing stability and opportunity for autistic workers.[148] One manager said it was important to "slowly [build] up the work role" to

---

[145] Hendricks, 2010, p. 128.

[146] Spoor, Bury, and Hedley, 2021.

[147] Stephanie R. Seitz and Sara A. Smith, "Working Toward Neurodiversity: How Organizations and Leaders Can Accommodate for Autism Spectrum Disorder," *Journal of Business and Management*, Vol. 22, No. 1, 2016.

[148] Dreaver et al., 2020.

continually challenge employees.[149] On the topic of building relationships in the workplace, the managers believed that it was essential for neurotypical employees to have an understanding of ASD. They felt this knowledge helped employees with ASD feel more welcome and more confident.[150]

[149] Dreaver et al., 2020, p. 1663.

[150] Dreaver et al., 2020.

Chapter 6. Recommendations and Conclusions for the U.S. Government

Government organizations that choose to embrace neurodiversity have several decisions to make, but at the core is a simple decision: Is their end goal to create a program specifically tailored for neurodivergent employees, or is it to embrace inclusivity by pivoting the entire organization to celebrate and embrace neurodiversity? We recommend the latter option for several reasons.

Interviews revealed that a program that is specifically tailored to neurodivergent employees faces several legal hurdles in the government. First, such a program would require applicants to self-identify as both neurodivergent and disabled. The benefit of such a program would be the ability to deliver targeted resources, interventions, and accommodations directly to the employees who need them and their immediate supervisors. However, self-disclosure requirements and targeted accommodations could create a "separate but equal" workforce in which the "separate" distinction opens the potential for bias, discrimination, and a sense of inadequacy. Second, agencies that have created similar programs have found it legally difficult to identify which jobs are being set aside for neurodivergent candidates. Our research and analysis indicates that neurodivergent employees should not be pigeonholed into specific positions but instead can be competitive for any type of career. Third, agencies that have created such pilot programs have identified some lessons that are transferrable across the organization but have also struggled to scale such programs across the entire workforce.[151]

> "It can't just be putting a bunch of fancy pamphlets together and saying, 'We're diverse!'"
>
> —Interview participant

On the other hand, if the organization's end goal is to embrace neurodiverse inclusivity—for all employees, regardless of cognitive classification—then no employees are singled out, and neurotypical employees can benefit from the same resources, interventions, and accommodations that are provided to neurodivergent employees.

Recommendations

There are several ways that government managers and leaders at various echelons could embrace neurodiversity, including low-cost or no-cost solutions that could be implemented immediately; along with longer-term solutions that could lead to systemic change across the

---

[151] The three hurdles described in this paragraph were derived from our firsthand experiences, and these experiences were corroborated in interviews.

national security enterprise. We focus these recommendations on those that can be agency-led—those that can be implemented within individual agencies—yet legislative or statutory changes could institutionalize these changes across the entire executive branch.

Provide All Employees Equally with Accommodations That Mitigate the Effects of Sensory Stimulation

Such accommodations might include the following:

- the ability to select or switch one's desk location in the office, appropriate to their grade, rank, or equivalent status, in order to move to a desk closer or further from an entrance, busy corridor, or other area of distraction
- the ability to change light bulbs above one's desk to reduce brightness or to remove a bulb completely
- access to noise-canceling headphones that are approved for use in the classified workspace
- the ability to request a fragrance-free or low-fragrance environment
- quiet times of day when interruptions or "drive-bys" will be minimized, except when necessary
- the ability to indicate—electronically on an Outlook calendar or physically with a sign on one's office door or cubicle entrance—a "do not interrupt" period of the day.

Modify Job Vacancies and Hiring Practices to Attract Neurodivergent Candidates

Changes could include the following:

- revising vacancy descriptions with more straightforward (less vague) language, removing jargon, and using job requirements that accurately reflect the needs of the position
- for vacancies, clearly identifying which requirements are co-occurring (applicant must have them all) versus independent (applicant needs only one on the list)
- revising the recruitment process to align with practices from organizations that recruit neurodivergent candidates.

In this area, the use of outside experts, including third-party organizations, could be helpful.

Help All Employees Understand Neurodiversity

Opportunities to build understanding include the following:

- inviting experts, especially those who identify as neurodivergent, to present on the topic of neurodiversity to groups in the organization
- making training on empathy and on creating environments for psychological safety (such as by raising awareness about tacit bias or unconscious discrimination, sometimes called *microaggressions*) required for all managers or providing new such training if it does not yet exist
- supporting agency affinity groups for neurodivergence that are not tied to disability but that exist independent of disability groups and encouraging these forums to become support networks and mentoring networks for employees across the organization.

Support Systemic Change Across the Organization

Along with these quick solutions, the following longer-term solutions could lead to systemic change across the national security enterprise:

- Engage with affinity groups to find individuals who could provide insights and perspectives to major policy deliberations, such as changes to agency telework or remote work policies, human resources policies, technology policies, and so on.
- In the security clearance process, examine ways to reduce the amount of paperwork, write clearer language in the SF-86, and better explain the process to applicants before they apply. Conduct research to examine whether and how the security clearance process, investigations, interviews, and polygraphs unintentionally discriminate against neurodivergent candidates, and examine options to train investigators and polygraph examiners about how neurodivergence may present in the clearance process and ways to mitigate such presentations on candidate adjudications.
- Examine military recruitment policies and practices (such as rules about ADD/ADHD medications) to identify options for increasing the pipeline of qualified candidates and to prevent otherwise qualified candidates from being weeded out. Military service creates a pipeline to all other national security careers through the use of veterans preference in hiring, so changes to military recruitment would affect all agencies across the enterprise.[152]
- Review and revise policies and practices in the military and other agencies that limit the deployment or overseas travel opportunities for neurodivergent employees. In national security, overseas assignments are an essential factor in promotion. Consider which policies can be removed or revised.

Readers can likely develop other recommendations based on the ideas presented in this report. We offer this list as a starting point, not as an end goal for the national security enterprise.

Conclusion

Now imagine a national security workplace that truly embraces neurodiversity. Positions are designed to allow each employee to bring their own skills and capabilities to the mission. Some people on the team excel at data mining, foreign languages, analysis, presentation skills, or interagency or international diplomacy. The team is a melting pot of cognitive approaches to problem-solving, communication, and analytics, in which each member of the team brings value to the collective good without being required to fit into a cookie-cutter mold. The terrific data scientist does not need to present results to a senior policymaker. The diplomat is not required to explain how the algorithm works.

This is a team that takes a truly multidisciplinary and *cognitive diversity* approach to analyzing foreign threats, solving acquisition challenges, developing and implementing new

---

[152] Frances Tilney Burke and Mackenzie Eaglen, "Is Veterans' Preference Bad for the National Security Workforce?" *War on the Rocks*, June 16, 2020.

hardware and software, conducting quality audits, strengthening U.S.-foreign relationships, and so on.

In this workplace, no one needs to disclose their neurodivergence in an interview to be evaluated for their strengths. Individuals are not put on performance improvement plans because they communicate differently or ask for more clarity. No one burns out after 18 months on the job because they have expended all their energy masking their neurodivergence. Employees have the option to select their desk in the office. The person who likes to be near the bathroom sits right in front of the SCIF door, while the person who needs few distractions chooses the far end of the room. Noise-canceling headphones and dimming light bulbs are available next to the notepads and pencils in the supply room; no special accommodation is necessary to pick up one of these items.

Managers are selected for emotional intelligence and empathy, and career tracks exist for technical experts who choose not to manage. Management training is consistent and valued and includes training on creating psychological safety and facilitating neurodiverse team dynamics. Managers mentor managers, employees mentor employees, and affinity groups create support systems for employees who seek them out.

Teams are performing at their highest potential, employees are proud of the agencies they work for, and special programs to "allow" neuro-inclusivity are completely unnecessary.

This imaginary world is not an impossible destination. The path to get there is composed of mostly small, simple steps taken by leaders—at all echelons—who are willing to begin.

Appendix A. Interview Protocol

RAND is conducting a study to examine the benefits and hurdles for employing persons with neurodiversity in knowledge workforces, and we will apply this research and analysis to the national security workforce. This research relies on publicly available and commercially available data, and we are focusing specifically on knowledge organizations, that means organizations that conduct analytic work comparable to national security professionals. Our goal is to examine the benefits and hurdles to employing persons with neurodiversity in national security roles.

Our research will address recruitment and hiring practices, managing employees, performance review processes, retention, and related topics. We strive to share lessons learned from other organizations that can benefit the government in its employment practices. The result of this project will be a publicly available publication sharing data and lessons.

We appreciate you participating in this study. This interview is voluntary. You are welcome to decline to participate or decline to answer any questions. We will not attribute specific comments or findings to specific individuals who we interviewed. We do not want you to share any PII-level information about specific employees in your organization. The goal of this interview is to capture themes and findings from your organization or your research, not to capture individual case examples.

Do you have any questions or concerns before we begin?

Introductory Questions

In our final report, we would like to acknowledge the people who contributed to this study. Do you grant permission for us to publish your name, title, and organization? You can still participate in this interview if you decline to be acknowledged in the report.

- Describe your current role (title, organization, job responsibilities)?
- Does your organization have a program specifically for neurodivergent employees? Describe your organization's relationship with neurodiversity in its workforce.

  - How many employees are in this group? What percent of the total workforce is that?
  - Are specific diagnoses included or excluded in this population? (e.g. autism spectrum (ASD), ADHD and ADD, Tourette's, other diagnoses)

Advantages and Challenges of a Neurodiverse Workforce

- What are the greatest advantages associated with increasing neurodiversity in your organization?

- What are the greatest disadvantages associated with increasing neurodiversity in your organization?

  – What costs—either financial, technology investments, or otherwise—has your organization experienced as a result of this program?

- Could you speak to any spillover effects you've noticed? For example, ways in which hiring neurodivergent individuals has improved the skills of managers or created challenges for management?
- Has your organization noticed different advantages or disadvantages for different forms of neurodivergence? For example, the advantages or disadvantages of ADHD vs. autism vs. dyslexia.
- We'd like to talk now about specific career fields within your organization. Are there specific career fields in which neurodivergent employees perform better or worse?

  – Which career fields?
  – Do you have hiring goals to seek neurodivergent candidates for any specific career fields? Why? Which career fields?
  – What type of data, metrics, or analytics has the organization used to come to these conclusions?

Hiring and Onboarding a Neurodiverse Workforce

- Walk us through the employee lifecycle for your neurodivergent workforce: from recruitment, hiring, on-boarding, managing and performance reviews, inter-office team dynamics, and so on. What is the lifecycle like for neurodivergent employees and how does this differ from the rest of the general workforce?

  – Are employees required to self-identify in order to access the benefits of this program or are the program benefits available to all employees evenly?
  – Are other colleagues aware that the member of their team or office is neurodivergent?

- What accommodations does your organization offer to neurodivergent persons during hiring and onboarding?

  – What accommodations did your organization try and discard? How do you assess the usefulness of an accommodation?

- How do you evaluate the effects of your neurodiversity hiring and onboarding program?

  – Have there been any changes your organization discarded after trying, or considered but found too difficult or costly to try?

- Do you have any plans to scale the program?

  – [If current program is autism-specific] Do you have any plans to expand this program – or develop new programs—for candidates and employees with dyslexia, ADHD, or other forms of neurodiversity?
  – How many employees (or what percentage of your workforce) do you plan to hire through this and related neurodiversity initiatives?

- Have you been able to continue recruiting neurodivergent candidates with consistent methods, or have you had to adjust your methods as the candidate pool changes? Do you anticipate being able to scale your current program as-is and still meet your hiring goals?

Managing and Retaining a Neurodiverse Workforce

- What accommodations does your organization offer to neurodivergent persons after a worker is brought on board?
  - Have you faced any challenges implementing these accommodations? Please share what they were and how you worked through those.
  - How have your existing employees responded to changes implemented to promote neurodiversity? Have these accommodations benefited them as well? Has there been any pushback from existing employees to changes you have made?
- What training do you provide to your managers and other employees in working with neurodivergent employees?
- How do you evaluate the effects of the accommodations and training you provide to promote neurodiversity?
  - Have there been any accommodations your organization discarded after trying, or considered but found too difficult or costly to try?

For Researchers:

- Are you aware of research on managing neurodiverse employees, including performance review processes and inter-team dynamics?

Closing Questions

- What have you learned that you wish you knew at the start of the program?
- Does your organization have any data, metrics, analytics, or reports that you can share with our team?
- What other topics should we discuss today?
- Who else or which other organizations should we be engaging with as part of this study?

Abbreviations

ADD	attention deficit disorder
ADHD	attention deficit hyperactivity disorder
ASD	autism spectrum disorder
CEO	chief executive officer
COVID-19	coronavirus disease 2019
DoD	U.S. Department of Defense
EEO	equal employment opportunity
EY	Ernst & Young
INSA	Intelligence and National Security Alliance
IT	information technology
NGA	National Geospatial-Intelligence Agency
SCIF	sensitive compartmented information facility
STEM	science, technology, engineering, and mathematics

References

Achievers Workforce Institute, *2022 Engagement and Retention Report: The Great Resignation Continues as Employees Seek Growth, Balance, and Support*, 2022.

Adams, Carol A., "Neurodiversity at Work Benefits Everyone—Why Companies Are Hiring Autistic People," *The Conversation*, September 24, 2020.

Agee, Kelly, and Alex Wilson, "Disabled People Fight US Military Disqualifications to Fulfill Their 'Duty to Serve,'" *Stars and Stripes*, April 21, 2022.

Alverson, Charlotte Y., Lauren E. Lindstrom, and Kara A. Hirano, "High School to College: Transition Experiences of Young Adults with Autism," *Focus on Autism and Other Developmental Disabilities*, Vol. 34, No. 1, March 2019.

Ameri, Mason, Lisa Schur, Meera Adya, F. Scott Bentley, Patrick McKay, and Douglas Kruse, "The Disability Employment Puzzle: A Field Experiment on Employer Hiring Behavior," *ILR Review*, Vol. 71, No. 2, March 2018.

Annabi, H., E. W. Crooks, N. Barnett, J. Guadagno, J. R. Mahoney, J. Michelle, A. Pacilio, H. Shukla, and J. Velasco, *Autism @ Work Playbook: Finding Talent and Creating Meaningful Employment Opportunities for People with Autism*, ACCESS-IT, The Information School, University of Washington, 2019.

Anonymous, "A Visible Career on the Spectrum," *Chemical Engineer*, February 27, 2020.

Aquino, Steven, "Google Cloud Exec Rob Enslin Talks Neurodiversity in the Workforce and How the Autism Career Program Seeks Top Talent," *Forbes*, July 26, 2021.

Austin, Robert D., Michael Fieldhouse, Aiyaswami Mohan, and Peter Quinn, "Why the Australian Defence Organization Is Recruiting Cyber Analysts on the Autism Spectrum," *Harvard Business Review*, December 7, 2017.

"Autistic Analysts Help U.S. Spy Agency," *CBS This Morning*, April 21, 2022. As of February 6, 2023:
https://www.cbs.com/shows/video/_XCOWqlrt7c6xXBE6GC0xIiHGTQlWhhx/

Baron-Cohen, Simon, "The Hyper-Systemizing, Assortative Mating Theory of Autism," *Progress in Neuro-Psychopharmacology and Biological Psychiatry*, Vol. 30, No. 5, July 2006.

Baron-Cohen, Simon, "Autism and the Technical Mind," *Scientific American*, Vol. 307, No. 5, November 2012.

Baron-Cohen, Simon, Emma Ashwin, Chris Ashwin, Teresa Tavassoli, and Bhismadev Chakrabarti, "Talent in Autism: Hyper-Systemizing, Hyper-Attention to Detail and Sensory Hypersensitivity," *Philosophical Transactions of the Royal Society B: Biological Sciences*, Vol. 364, No. 1522, May 27, 2009.

Bernick, Michael, "Is Your Company Inclusive of Neurodivergent Employees?" *Harvard Business Review*, February 16, 2022.

Bilokonsky, Mykola, "How to Talk About Autism Respectfully," Public Neurodiversity Support Center, December 19, 2021. As of February 6, 2023: https://coda.io/@mykola-bilokonsky/public-neurodiversity-support-center/how-to-talk-about-autism-respectfully-84

Budryk, Zack, "More Celebrities Are Coming Out as Autistic. That Makes a Huge Difference," *Washington Post*, September 8, 2021.

Camarena, Phame M., and Pamela A. Sarigiani, "Postsecondary Educational Aspirations of High-Functioning Adolescents with Autism Spectrum Disorders and Their Parents," *Focus on Autism and Other Developmental Disabilities*, Vol. 24, No. 2, June 2009.

Carucci, Ron, "To Retain New Hires, Spend More Time Onboarding Them," *Harvard Business Review*, December 3, 2018.

Centers for Disease Control and Prevention, "Data & Statistics on Autism Spectrum Disorder," webpage, last reviewed March 2, 2022a. As of February 6, 2023: https://www.cdc.gov/ncbddd/autism/data.html

Centers for Disease Control and Prevention, "Signs and Symptoms of Autism Spectrum Disorder," webpage, last reviewed March 28, 2022b. As of February 6, 2023: https://www.cdc.gov/ncbddd/autism/signs.html

Central Intelligence Agency, "Accountant," webpage, undated. As of April 15, 2022: https://www.cia.gov/careers/jobs/accountant/

Centre for Excellence in Universal Design, "What Is Universal Design," webpage, undated. As of September 14, 2022: https://universaldesign.ie/what-is-universal-design

Chevallier, Coralie, Gregor Kohls, Vanessa Troiani, Edward S. Brodkin, and Robert T. Schultz, "The Social Motivation Theory of Autism," *Trends in Cognitive Sciences*, Vol. 16, No. 4, April 2012.

Collins, Erika C., and Emilee Schipske, "Global Neurodiversity: A Workplace Primer on Attracting and Retaining Neurodiverse Talent," *LaborSphere*, blog, July 26, 2021. As of February 6, 2023:
https://laborsphere.com/global-neurodiversity-a-workplace-primer-on-attracting-and-retaining-neurodiverse-talent/

Comaford, Christine, "Is Neurodiversity the Right Talent Path for Your Organization?" *Forbes*, June 24, 2017.

Cook, Gareth, "The Autism Advantage," *New York Times Magazine*, November 29, 2012.

Cooper, Anderson, "Recruiting for Talent on the Autism Spectrum," *60 Minutes*, July 18, 2021.

Cunningham, Maria, "Barriers to the Diagnosis of Dyslexia in Children," *Yale Undergraduate Research Journal*, Vol. 2, No. 1, Spring 2021.

Curry Hall, Kimberly, Kirsten M. Keller, David Schulker, Sarah Weilant, Katherine L. Kidder, and Nelson Lim, *Improving Gender Diversity in the U.S. Coast Guard: Identifying Barriers to Female Retention*, Homeland Security Operational Analysis Center operated by the RAND Corporation, RR-2770-DHS, 2019. As of January 12, 2023:
https://www.rand.org/pubs/research_reports/RR2770.html

Dai, Guangrong, and Kenneth P. De Meuse, "A Review of Onboarding Literature," Lominger Limited, January 12, 2007.

Danielson, Melissa L., Rebecca H. Bitsko, Reem M. Ghandour, Joseph R. Holbrook, Michael D. Kogan, and Stephen J. Blumberg, "Prevalence of Parent-Reported ADHD Diagnosis and Associated Treatment Among U.S. Children and Adolescents, 2016," *Journal of Clinical Child & Adolescent Psychology*, Vol. 47, No. 2, March–April 2018.

Davis, Hazel, "Forget Stereotypes . . . How to Recruit Talented, Neurodiverse Employees," *The Guardian*, August 31, 2017.

Davis, Tre, "Airman Advocates for Neurodiversity in Military," U.S. Air Force, August 6, 2021.

Day-Duro, Emma, Grace Brown, and Julian Thompson, *Thinking Differently: Neurodiversity in the Workplace*, HULT International Business School, undated.

Devlin-Rutgers, Dory, "Employers Show Bias Against People with Disabilities," *Futurity*, January 5, 2016.

DoD—*See* U.S. Department of Defense.

Dow, Mirah J., Brady D. Lund, and William K. Douthit, "Investigating the Link Between Unemployment and Disability: Lexically Ambiguous Words and Fixed Formulaic Sequences in Job Ads for Academic Reference Librarians," *International Journal of Information, Diversity, & Inclusion*, Vol. 4, No. 1, 2020.

Dreaver, Jessica, Craig Thompson, Sonya Girdler, Margareta Adolfsson, Melissa H. Black, and Marita Falkmer, "Success Factors Enabling Employment for Adults on the Autism Spectrum from Employers' Perspective," *Journal of Autism and Developmental Disorders*, Vol. 50, No. 5, May 2020.

Employer Assistance and Resource Network on Disability Inclusion, "Neurodiversity in the Workplace," webpage, undated. As of April 15, 2022: https://askearn.org/page/neurodiversity-in-the-workplace

Ernst & Young, "EY US Launches First Neuro-Diverse Center of Excellence in Boston," press release, April 12, 2021.

Ernst & Young, "EY Achieves Highest Growth in Nearly Two Decades, Reports Record Global Revenue of US$45.4b," press release, September 21, 2022.

Executive Order 13985, *Advancing Racial Equity and Support for Underserved Communities Through the Federal Government*, White House, January 20, 2021.

Executive Order 14035, *Diversity, Equity, Inclusion, and Accessibility in the Federal Workforce*, White House, June 25, 2021.

EY—*See* Ernst & Young.

Faram, Mark D., "Sweeping Uniform Changes Emphasize Gender Neutrality," *Navy Times*, October 9, 2015.

Florey, Anna T., and David A. Harrison, "Responses to Informal Accommodation Requests from Employees with Disabilities: Multistudy Evidence on Willingness to Comply," *Academy of Management Journal*, Vol. 43, No. 2, April 2000.

Gale, Adam, "Why Linklaters Is Hiring Neurodiverse People," Management Today, updated September 24, 2020.

Goldman Sachs, "Neurodiversity Hiring Initiative," webpage, undated. As of March 23, 2022: https://www.goldmansachs.com/careers/professionals/neurodiversity-hiring-initiative.html

Gonzalez, Cleotilde, Jolie M. Martin, Nancy J. Minshew, and Marlene Behrmann, "Practice Makes Improvement: How Adults with Autism Out-Perform Others in a Naturalistic Visual Search Task," *Journal of Autism and Developmental Disorders*, Vol. 43, No. 10, October 2013.

Hartness, M. Suzanne, and John D. Bowers, "Neurodiversity in the Practice of Law," *Law Practice Magazine*, November 1, 2020.

Harvey, India, Samuela Bolgan, Daniel Mosca, Colin McLean, and Elena Rusconi, "Systemizers Are Better Code-Breakers: Self-Reported Systemizing Predicts Code-Breaking Performance in Expert Hackers and Naïve Participants," *Frontiers in Human Neuroscience*, Vol. 10, May 17, 2016.

Henderson, William, "Mental Health and Final Security Clearances," ClearanceJobs, March 29, 2022.

Hendricks, Dawn, "Employment and Adults with Autism Spectrum Disorders: Challenges and Strategies for Success," *Journal of Vocational Rehabilitation*, Vol. 32, No. 2, 2010.

Hogan, Toschia M., and Joseph Liu, "Status Is the Difference: Disability and the Unintended Consequences of Fairness," *Academy of Management Proceedings*, Vol. 2018, No. 1, 2018.

Horowitz, Julia, "Goldman Sachs Plans to Hire More Neurodiverse Employees, Including People on the Autism Spectrum," *CNN Business*, April 2, 2019.

Hotez, Emily, Christina Shane-Simpson, Rita Obeid, Danielle DeNigris, Michael Siller, Corinna Costikas, Jonathan Pickens, Anthony Massa, Michael Giannola, Joanne D'Onofrio, and Kristen Gillespie-Lynch, "Designing a Summer Transition Program for Incoming and Current College Students on the Autism Spectrum: A Participatory Approach," *Frontiers in Psychology*, Vol. 9, February 13, 2018.

Horvath, Frank S., and John E. Reid, "The Polygraph Silent Answer Test," *Journal of Criminal Law, Criminology, and Police Science*, Vol. 63, No. 2, June 1972.

Hu, Yang, Alessandra M. Pereira, Xiaoxue Gao, Brunno M. Campos, Edmund Derrington, Brice Corgnet, Xiaolin Zhou, Fernando Cendes, and Jean-Claude Dreher, "Right Temporoparietal Junction Underlies Avoidance of Moral Transgression in Autism Spectrum Disorder," *Journal of Neuroscience*, Vol. 41, No. 8, February 24, 2021.

Hurlbutt, Karen, and Lynne Chalmers, "Employment and Adults with Asperger Syndrome," *Focus on Autism and Other Developmental Disabilities*, Vol. 19, No. 4, Winter 2004.

Julian, Anna, and Ronda Barron, "Employees with Asperger's Syndrome and Their Experiences Within the Work Environment," *DBS Business Review,* Vol. 3, 2019.

Karpinski, Ruth I., Audrey M. Kinase Kolb, Nicole A. Tetreault, and Thomas B. Borowski, "High Intelligence: A Risk Factor for Psychological and Physiological Overexcitabilities," *Intelligence*, Vol. 66, January–February 2018.

LethalityJane, "It's pretty much common knowledge in a lot of technical military MOS's that a bunch of our peers have undiagnosed ADHD or Autism," Twitter post, June 23, 2022. As of February 6, 2023:
https://twitter.com/LethalityJane/status/1540119983849558016

Lewington, Jennifer, "In the Global Hunt for Tech-Savvy Workers, Companies Are Turning to a Once-Ignored Source of Talent: Those Diagnosed with Autism," *Globe and Mail*, February 25, 2021.

Lim, Alliyza, Robyn L. Young, and Neil Brewer, "Autistic Adults May Be Erroneously Perceived as Deceptive and Lacking Credibility," *Journal of Autism and Developmental Disorders*, Vol. 52, No. 2, February 2022.

Lundberg, J. C. [@jclundberg], "The nuclear Navy would fail if we had comprehensive autism testing in the accessions pipeline," Twitter post, June 23, 2022. As of February 6, 2023: https://twitter.com/jclundberg/status/1540142770748133376

Maras, Katie, "What to Do When Interviewing an Autistic Person for a Job?" University of Bath, undated.

Maras, Katie, Sue Mulcahy, Laura Crane, Tamsyn Hawken, and Amina Memon, "Obtaining Best Evidence from the Autistic Interviewee: Police-Reported Challenges, Legal Requirements and Psychological Research-Based Recommendations," *Investigative Interviewing: Research and Practice*, Vol. 9, No. 1, 2018.

Maras, Katie, Jade Eloise Norris, Jemma Nicholson, Brett Heasman, Anna Remington, and Laura Crane, "Ameliorating the Disadvantage for Autistic Job Seekers: An Initial Evaluation of Adapted Employment Interview Questions," *Autism*, Vol. 25, No. 4, May 2021.

McMahon, Camilla M., Stacey Henry, and Meghan Linthicum, "Employability in Autism Spectrum Disorder (ASD): Job Candidate's Diagnostic Disclosure and ASD Characteristics and Employer's ASD Knowledge and Social Desirability," *Journal of Experimental Psychology: Applied*, Vol. 27, No. 1, March 2021.

Merriam-Webster, "Executive Function," webpage, undated. As of February 6, 2023: https://www.merriam-webster.com/dictionary/executive%20function

Milton, Damian E. M., "On the Ontological Status of Autism: the 'Double Empathy Problem,'" *Disability & Society*, Vol. 27, No. 6, October 2012.

Mintz, Luke, and Dominic Penna, "'Once I'm Focused on a Task, I Won't Stop': Why Employers Are Hiring More Autistic People," *The Telegraph*, January 28, 2020.

Morris, Meredith Ringel, Andrew Begel, and Ben Wiedermann, "Understanding the Challenges Faced by Neurodiverse Software Engineering Employees: Towards a More Inclusive and Productive Technical Workforce," *Proceedings of ASSETS 2015*, October 2015.

Mottron, Laurent, "Changing Perceptions: The Power of Autism," *Nature,* Vol. 479, November 3, 2011.

Müller, Eve, Adriana Schuler, Barbara A. Burton, and Gregory B. Yates, "Meeting the Vocational Support Needs of Individuals with Asperger Syndrome and Other Autism Spectrum Disabilities," *Journal of Vocational Rehabilitation*, Vol. 18, No. 3, 2003.

National Institute of Mental Health, "Autism Spectrum Disorder," webpage, undated. As of February 6, 2023:
https://www.nimh.nih.gov/health/topics/autism-spectrum-disorders-asd

National Geospatial-Intelligence Agency, "NGA Launches Neurodiversity Pilot," press release, January 13, 2021.

NotchbackFiero, "I'll get tested after I retire. Not worth losing my wings over, unfortunately," Twitter post, June 24, 2022. As of February 6, 2023:
https://twitter.com/NotchbackFiero/status/1540520131830468615

Ogrysko, Nicole, "Biden Calls for Agency Ideas to Win the Race for National Security Talent," *Federal News Network*, February 5, 2021.

Paetzold, Ramona L., María Fernanda García, Adrienne Colella, Lily Run Ren, María del Carmen Triana, and Monique Ziebro, "Perceptions of People with Disabilities: When Is Accommodation Fair?" *Basic and Applied Social Psychology*, Vol. 30, 2008.

Papasmurf811, "Some of us are diagnosed. The military just dosen't know it. I was told by my recruiter not to mention it at MEPS." Twitter post, June 23, 2022. As of February 21, 2023:
https://twitter.com/Papasmurf811/status/1540185745767518208

Parr, Alissa D., Samuel T. Hunter, and Gina Scott Ligon, "Questioning Universal Applicability of Transformational Leadership: Examining Employees with Autism Spectrum Disorder," *Leadership Quarterly*, Vol. 24, No. 4, August 2013.

Patton, Eric, "Autism, Attributions and Accommodations: Overcoming Barriers and Integrating a Neurodiverse Workforce," *Personnel Review*, Vol. 48, No. 4, 2019.

Payne, Katy-Louise, Ailsa Russell, Richard Mills, Katie Maras, Dheeraj Rai, and Mark Brosnan, "Is There a Relationship Between Cyber-Dependent Crime, Autistic-Like Traits and Autism?" *Journal of Autism and Developmental Disorders*, Vol. 49, No. 10, October 2019.

Pellicano, Elizabeth, Murray Maybery, Kevin Durkin, and Alana Maley, "Multiple Cognitive Capabilities/Deficits in Children with an Autism Spectrum Disorder: 'Weak' Central Coherence and Its Relationship to Theory of Mind and Executive Control," *Development and Psychopathology*, Vol. 18, No. 1, March 2006.

Polaneczky, Ronnie, "A 'Rich Ecosystem of Support' for Adults with Autism Led to One Young Employee Filing Two Patents for SAP," *Philadelphia Inquirer*, November 13, 2019.

powerswf, "I was diagnosed with ADHD as a FGO; prior enlisted SIGINT/Russian linguist. The military thrives because of us with ADHD. It's asinine to think they are screening people because of it. The only reason I got in is because us Gen-Xers never went to the doctor pre-military," Twitter post, June 23, 2022. As of February 6, 2023:
https://twitter.com/powerswf/status/1540148379732172802

Rafferty, Alannah E., and Mark A. Griffin, "Dimensions of Transformational Leadership: Conceptual and Empirical Extensions," *Leadership Quarterly*, Vol. 15, No. 3, June 2004.

Ren, Lily Run, Ramona L. Paetzold, and Adrienne Colella, "A Meta-Analysis of Experimental Studies on the Effects of Disability on Human Resource Judgments," *Human Resource Management Review*, Vol. 18, No. 3, September 2008.

Robertson, Marcella, "Navy Rescinds Student's ROTC Scholarship Because of His Autism Diagnosis," *WUSA*, June 18, 2021.

Romualdez, Anna Melissa, Zachary Walker, and Anna Remington, "Autistic Adults' Experiences of Diagnostic Disclosure in the Workplace: Decision-Making and Factors Associated with Outcomes," *Autism & Developmental Language Impairments*, Vol. 6, 2021.

Rovnick, Naomi, "Hiring More 'Neurodiverse' Workers Can Pay Dividends," *Financial Times*, November 20, 2019.

Rubin, Shira, "The Israeli Army Unit That Recruits Teens with Autism," *The Atlantic*, January 6, 2016.

Ruef, Michael B., and Ann P. Turnbull, "The Perspectives of Individuals with Cognitive Disabilities and/or Autism on Their Lives and Their Problem Behavior," *Research and Practice for Persons with Severe Disabilities*, Vol. 27, No. 2, June 2002.

Ryan, Ann Marie, and Robert E. Ployhart, "A Century of Selection," *Annual Review of Psychology*, Vol. 65, January 2014.

Sacks, Oliver, *An Anthropologist on Mars: Seven Paradoxical Tales*, Knopf, 1995.

Samuel, Alexandra, "As Remote Work Becomes the Norm, Vast New Possibilities Open for Autistic People," *Wall Street Journal*, March 8, 2021.

SAP SE, *SAP Integrated Report 2021*, 2022.

Sardon, Maitane, "How Microsoft Tapped the Autism Community for Talent," *Wall Street Journal*, October 26, 2019.

Schaefer, Agnes Gereben, Jennie W. Wenger, Jennifer Kavanagh, Jonathan P. Wong, Gillian S. Oak, Thomas E. Trail, and Todd Nichols, *Implications of Integrating Women into the Marine Corps Infantry*, RAND Corporation, RR-1103-USMC, 2015. As of January 12, 2023:
https://www.rand.org/pubs/research_reports/RR1103.html

Schoenberg, Nara, "'We Don't Care About the Eye Contact.' Autistic People Thrive in Chicago Tech Jobs After Years of Underemployment," *Chicago Tribune*, June 11, 2019.

Scott, Melissa, Andrew Jacob, Delia Hendrie, Richard Parsons, Sonya Girdler, Torbjörn Falkmer, and Marita Falkmer, "Employers' Perception of the Costs and the Benefits of Hiring Individuals with Autism Spectrum Disorder in Open Employment in Australia," *PloS ONE*, Vol. 12, No. 5, May 18, 2017.

Scott-Van Zeeland, Ashley A., Mirella Dapretto, Dara G. Ghahremani, Russell A. Poldrack, and Susan Y. Bookheimer, "Reward Processing in Autism," *Autism Research*, Vol. 3, No. 2, April 2010.

Seitz, Stephanie R., and Sara A. Smith, "Working Toward Neurodiversity: How Organizations and Leaders Can Accommodate for Autism Spectrum Disorder," *Journal of Business and Management*, Vol. 22, No. 1, 2016.

Shein, Esther, "Hiring from the Autism Spectrum," *Communications of the ACM*, Vol. 63, No. 6, June 2020.

Silberman, Steve, *NeuroTribes: The Legacy of Autism and the Future of Neurodiversity*, Avery, 2015.

Singleton, Kaela S., De-Shaine R. K. Murray, Angeline J. Dukes, and Lietsel N. S. Richardson, "A Year in Review: Are Diversity, Equity, and Inclusion Initiatives Fixing Systemic Barriers?" *NeuroView*, Vol. 109, No. 21, November 3, 2021.

Soulières, Isabelle, Michelle Dawson, Fabienne Samson, Elise B. Barbeau, Chérif P. Sahyoun, Gary E. Strangman, Thomas A. Zeffiro, and Laurent Mottron, "Enhanced Visual Processing Contributes to Matrix Reasoning in Autism," *Human Brain Mapping*, Vol. 30, No. 12, December 2009.

Sperry, Laurie A., and Gary B. Mesibov, "Perceptions of Social Challenges of Adults with Autism Spectrum Disorder," *Autism*, Vol. 9, No. 4, October 2005.

Spoor, Jennifer R., Simon M. Bury, and Darren Hedley, "Non-Autistic Employees' Perspectives on the Implementation of an Autism Employment Programme," *Autism*, Vol. 25, No. 8, November 2021.

Szulc, Joanna Maria, Julie A. Davies, Michał T. Tomczak, and Frances-Louise McGregor, "AMO Perspectives on the Well-Being of Neurodivergent Human Capital," *Employee Relations*, Vol. 43, No. 4, 2021.

Tilney Burke, Frances, and Mackenzie Eaglen, "Is Veterans' Preference Bad for the National Security Workforce?" *War on the Rocks*, June 16, 2020.

Tomczak, Michał T., "Employees with Autism Spectrum Disorders in the Digitized Work Environment: Perspectives for the Future," *Journal of Disability Policy Studies*, Vol. 31, No. 4, March 2021.

Tzul, Richard, "Growing EY Initiative Promotes Workplace Neurodiversity," Bloomberg Tax, June 13, 2022.

USA Jobs, "Contracting Officer Representative, Department of Defense, Missile Defense Agency," Announcement No. MDA-21-11170262-DH-OC, Control No. 608656900, accessed June 22, 2022a.

USA Jobs, "Program Analyst (Cyber Operations), Department of the Air Force, Air Combat Command," Announcement No. s-22-DHA-11223362-JLE, Control No. 616240500, accessed June 22, 2022b.

USA Jobs, "Business Analyst (Data Modeler/Metadata Specialist/Open Government Data Specialist), Federal Reserve System," Announcement No. DEST-11485818-22-CB, Control No. 652648400, accessed July 15, 2022c.

U.S. Department of Defense, Office of the Deputy Assistant Secretary of Defense for Military Community and Family Policy, *2020 Demographics: Profile of the Military Community*, 2021.

U.S. Department of Homeland Security, "About DHS," webpage, updated April 5, 2022. As of July 27, 2022:
https://www.dhs.gov/about-dhs

U.S. Department of Labor, "Schedule A Letter," undated. As of July 19, 2022:
https://www.dol.gov/sites/dolgov/files/odep/pdf/schedule_a_sample_letter.pdf

U.S. Department of Labor, Office of Disability Employment Policy, "Accommodations," webpage, undated. As of April 7, 2022:
https://www.dol.gov/agencies/odep/program-areas/employers/accommodations

U.S. Department of State, "About the U.S. Department of State," webpage, undated. As of July 27, 2022:
https://www.state.gov/about/

U.S. Naval Academy, "Appendix A: Medical Considerations for Admissions," undated.

U.S. Office of Personnel Management, "Reasonable Accommodation," webpage, undated. As of February 6, 2023:
https://www.opm.gov/policy-data-oversight/employee-relations/reasonable-accommodation/

U.S. Office of Personnel Management, "Self-Identification of Disability," SF 256, revised October 2016.

Van Loon, Ronald, "How to Become a Data Modeler in 2023?" Simplilearn, updated January 31, 2023.

Vincent, Jonathan, "Employability for UK University Students and Graduates on the Autism Spectrum: Mobilities and Materialities," *Scandinavian Journal of Disability Research*, Vol. 22, No. 1, 2020.

Vrabel, Rob, "Can You Join the Military with Autism?" Operation Military Kids, June 7, 2021.

Walkowiak, Emmanuelle, "Neurodiversity of the Workforce and Digital Transformation: The Case of Inclusion of Autistic Workers at the Workplace," *Technological Forecasting and Social Change*, Vol. 168, July 2021.

Wang, Shirley S., "How Autism Can Help You Land a Job," *Wall Street Journal*, March 27, 2014.

White, Tracie, "Stanford Program Matches Autistic Job Seekers with Employers," Stanford Medicine, November 5, 2021.

WildAlaskanRed, "Add me to the list. I excelled as both an Apache crew chief and an EOD tech. The technical skill required was easy. The Army gave me structure so I didn't realize I had problems until I left," Twitter post, June 24, 2022a. As of February 6, 2023: https://twitter.com/WildAlaskanRed/status/1540430884343427073

WildAlaskanRed, "Add to that my ability to hyper-focus. EOD is the perfect job for someone with ADHD," Twitter post, June 24, 2022b. As of February 6, 2023: https://twitter.com/WildAlaskanRed/status/1540431593138839552

Wood, Vincent, "GCHQ Targeting Dyslexic and Neurodiverse People in Recruitment Drive, Spy Chief Says," *Independent*, October 21, 2019.

Zedeck, Sheldon, ed., *APA Handbook of Industrial and Organizational Psychology:* Vol. 2, *Selecting and Developing Members for the Organization*, American Psychological Association, 2011.